CAMPUS MINISTRY
COLLEGE OF ST. BENEDICT
ST. JOSEPH, MN 56374

CHOOSING

CASES IN
MORAL
DECISION-MAKING

D1413855

CHOOSING

CASES IN
MORAL
DECISION-MAKING

Michael Pennock

AVE MARIA PRESS   Notre Dame, Indiana 46556

Nihil Obstat: The Reverend Gerald J. Bednar, J.D., Ph.D.
Censor Deputatus

Imprimatur: The Most Reverend Anthony M. Pilla, D.D., M.A.
Bishop of Cleveland

Given at Cleveland, Ohio on 29 October 1990.

The *Nihil Obstat* and *Imprimatur* are official declarations that a book or pamphlet is free of doctrinal or moral error. No implication is contained therein that those who have granted the *Nihil Obstat* and *Imprimatur* agree with the contents, opinions, or statements expressed.

Excerpts from THE DOCUMENTS OF VATICAN II, Abbott-Gallagher edition, reprinted with permission of America Press, Inc., 106 West 56th Street, New York, NY 10019. © 1966 All Rights Reserved.

Excerpts from THE NEW JERUSALEM BIBLE, copyright © 1985 by Darton, Longman & Todd, Ltd. and Doubleday & Company, Inc. Reprinted by permission of the publisher.

© 1991 by Ave Maria Press, Notre Dame, IN 46556

All rights reserved. No part of this book may be used or reproduced in any manner whatsoever without written permission, except in the case of reprints in the context of reviews.

International Standard Book Number: 0-87793-446-0

Library of Congress Catalog Card Number: 90-85155

Cover and text design by Katherine Robinson Coleman

Printed and bound in the United States of America.

Contents

Introduction

How would you answer this question: **"Should there be a dual minimum wage law?"** The purpose of the law would be to allow employers to hire unemployed teens at less than minimum wage to help alleviate high unemployment among youth, especially among minorities.

This question presents a real moral *quandary*, a word the dictionary defines as "a state of uncertainty or perplexity." Synonyms include words like *dilemma*, *predicament*, and *plight*. A little bit of reflection reveals that life is full of quandaries. How would you approach the minimum-wage dilemma if you have a decent summer job that allows you to save money for college yet spend some on yourself? How would you answer it if you simply could not find a job, no matter how hard you tried? Many employers have said they would hire more youth if the standard minimum wage were not so high. Would they actually do so? Would a dual wage enable unscrupulous employers to take advantage of relatively defenseless teens? The answers to these questions are not easy.

Not all dilemmas are this tough nor do they involve grave social consequences. Many are relatively minor or insignificant. For example, suppose one set of friends wants you to go to the school football game on Friday night while another group wants you to go to the movies. What should you do? Both alternatives are attractive. You enjoy the company of both sets of friends. Regardless of how you resolve this predicament, no great moral issues are involved. Your life won't radically change one way or another.

However, other personal quandaries are more difficult and involve moral choices. For example, should you cheat on the exam when everyone else is? Other dilemmas involve life choices. Suppose, for example, you have the talent and interest to study both law and medicine. You are attracted to both possibilities. Which one should you pursue? Still other situations involve our relationship with God. For example, the book of Revelation quotes the risen Jesus:

> "I know...how you are neither cold nor hot. I wish
> you were one or the other, but since you are neither
> hot nor cold, but only lukewarm, I will spit you out of
> my mouth" (Rv 3:15).

Every Christian is faced with the dilemma Revelation alludes to: How committed should we be as followers of Jesus? How much should we love him, and how should this love figure in the way we live our lives?

Resolving quandaries requires making decisions. Deciding means getting off dead center. As Revelation graphically reminds us, lukewarmness is an evasion. It is not a true decision because it doesn't commit us to a definite course of action. It really doesn't solve anything. The dilemma remains.

This book presents many moral dilemmas and situations to help you sort out your values and think about the many issues involved in making moral decisions. It is a *resource book* for reflection on and analysis of personal values. It is also a *casebook* that includes many problems and situations. It offers sound decision-making techniques and principles that will help you discuss some interesting and real moral issues that intelligent Christians are concerned about today. These issues include situations in Christian living, bioethical dilemmas, and topics in justice.

The book is written from a Catholic-Christian perspective. Its basic premise is that the Lord Jesus offers abundant life. His teaching, example, and friendship have helped countless people over the centuries to live productive, happy, and loving lives. The book also looks to the teachings of the Catholic church as a reliable resource for living a Christian, moral life in harmony with Jesus' call to fullness of life.

How to use this book

Since this book has a casebook format, you can use each exercise independently of the others. Skip around if you want. Page through the book to see what types of issues are taken up. However, you may wish to read the introductions to each section to see what the exercises in that category are about.

Here are four easy rules to help you work through these exercises:

Rule 1: **Gather information.**   You can't go wrong keeping an open mind and learning as much as you can about your particular dilemma. The educated person doesn't have to fear knowledge.

However, there are many different voices in today's society competing for your attention and your allegiance. Consider the following:

> Psychology says...Be self-analytical, fulfill yourself.
> Consumerism says...Be acquisitive, indulge yourself.
> Secularism says...Be realistic, rely on yourself alone.
> The Playgirl/Playboy approach says...Be sensuous, enjoy yourself.
> Athleticism says...Be strong, discipline yourself.
> Jesus says...Love God above everything and your neighbor as yourself.

Which voices should you believe? Who is worth paying attention to? The second rule will help here.

Rule 2: **Ask questions.**   A college professor once promised his students an A in his course if they asked just one intelligent question. Knowledge is about asking questions as well as giving answers. A Chinese proverb puts it well: "He who asks a question is a fool for five minutes; he who does not ask a question remains a fool forever."

Take the time to ask questions of yourself and others. The right question can make all the difference. Instead of swallowing consumerism's advice, we might ask: "What happens if I always indulge myself?" Or we might ask the playboy: "What does a sensuous lifestyle bring me?" And, we can even ask Jesus: "Is love truly the key to happiness?"

Questions are fun and absolutely necessary for intellectual and moral growth.

Rule 3: **Discuss.**   The exercises in this book are designed for easy discussion with your peers, friends, group leader, parents, teachers, etc. Discussion is a mind-broadening learning technique. It teaches us that no one has all the truth and that everyone has some aspect of the truth from which we can learn. In your discussions, try to do the following:

- *Allow others to express themselves freely in a friendly atmosphere.* As our brothers and sisters in the Lord, others deserve respectful attention.
- *Really listen to what others are saying.* Even if it contradicts your own thoughts and feelings, try to see the issue from the viewpoint of the person speaking. The philosopher Arthur Schopenhauer said, "Compassion is the basis of all morality." Some may dispute this, but most of us could agree that compassion ("feeling with") must be at the heart of all true dialogue.
- *Separate fact from feeling and opinion.*
- *Say what you really think and feel, not what you think others want to hear.* Be your own person. Your courage to speak the truth can be immensely helpful to others.
- *Have fun.* Don't be so deadly serious that you can't laugh at yourself or see the many incongruities in life. We learn from our mistakes.

Rule 4: **Decide.**   Eventually you must reach a point where you're "discussed out." You've asked all the questions and done all the research. It is time to decide, to answer the question, to choose the value.

An advantage of a book like this is that it allows you to discuss moral dilemmas with friends and concerned adults in a safe and non-threatening way. It rehearses potentially troublesome problems and issues *before* they arise in your own life. It can help you sort through your values, hear what Jesus and the church say, and consider calmly many important issues.

You can always change your mind. Change, by the way, is a sign of growth. The famous British statesman Sir Winston Churchill once said, "A fanatic is one who can't change his mind and won't change the subject."

Be brave enough to change your mind when you are wrong and bold enough to make your prayer that of the famous theologian Reinhold Niebuhr:

> God, give us grace to accept with serenity the things
> that cannot be changed, courage to change the things
> which should be changed, and the wisdom to distin-
> guish the one from the other. *The Serenity Prayer* (1938)

May God bless you on your journey through these moral quandaries.

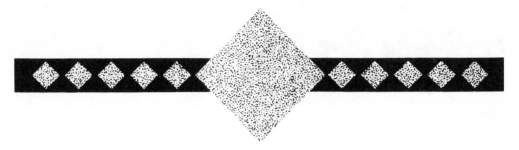

section one

Values

The dictionary defines the word *value* this way: "A principle, standard or quality considered worthwhile or desirable." Tell me your values and you reveal yourself—what you hope for, what is important to you, how you view life. For some, reputation is more valuable than money. For others, time outweighs all other considerations. Still others claim that the truth outranks everything. And, of course, there are countless other values that people hold dear, values that affect their lives and relationships with others.

Something is of value to us if we—

- prize and cherish it
- choose it freely from among alternatives after considering the consequences of each
- affirm it publicly
- act on it repeatedly

The following exercises are designed to help you discover your values so you can look at them critically and examine how they influence the important moral choices that life presents.

Reflect, discuss, share, and have fun working through these exercises. You may surprise yourself as you look deeply into the mysterious person you are.

1. Asking Questions

James Thurber once observed that "it is better to know some of the questions than all of the answers."

Here are some questions to help you determine some of your key values. Write a short response to them and then discuss your answers in small groups of four.

1. Suppose a philanthropist gave you $100,000 to give to your three favorite charities. You have one week to dispose of the money. Which worthy causes would you pick and why?

a.

b.

c.

2. Are you a follower or a leader?

3. Would you rather lose the ability to talk or the sense of hearing?

CHOOSING

a. If you said the ability to talk, who would be the last person you'd like to talk to?

b. If you said hearing, what is the last sound you'd like to hear?

4. What is your worst bad habit? What first step should you take toward overcoming it?

5. What one saint would you most like to meet, and what would you like to ask him or her?

6. If you knew you were to die in three months, what three things would you change about yourself starting now?

a.

b.

c.

7. What would you like the priest to say at your funeral?

8. Would you rather play tennis with someone slightly more or less talented than you?

9. Would you rather be in a class where your fellow students are smarter or slightly less talented than you?

10. What person would you most like to meet? What would you ask this · person?

11. What do you admire most about your parents?

father:

mother:

12. Have you ever thought of a vocation to the religious life? What would you say if a priest or sister told you that you'd make a good religious?

13. What is your greatest achievement to date? What goal would you like to reach in the next five years?

14. At what career would you most like to be successful? Define success.

15. Suppose someone breaks into your house and steals everything. However, the burglar allows you to keep one thing. What would you choose?

16. If you were to die tonight, how would you like to spend the rest of your day?

17. Would you rather be successful at sports or at making friends?

CHOOSING

18. Would you have participated in an assassination attempt on Hitler's life knowing that its chances of success were only fifty percent?

■ *exercises* ■

a. In your journal, list three new things you learned about yourself by asking yourself these questions.

b. In general, do you seem to value things or people more? Explain.

2. Your Honesty Quotient

One of the first values most people think about in dealing with others is honesty. No relationship can survive unless it is based on honesty. Some questions involving honesty are easy, for example, Would you steal ten dollars from your dad's billfold? Others are more difficult. How would you deal with the following situations?

1. Would you ask one of your parents to call your school to say you are sick so you could stay home to finish a school project? Would this be lying?

2. A friend of yours asks you to read his essay. It is terrible. He will be hurt if you tell the truth. How will you handle this situation?

3. Would you lie for a friend? If yes, under what circumstances? If not, why not? What if he or she offered you $100 to lie?

4. You bought some items in a five-and-dime store, and you notice that the clerk did not charge you for all of them. Would you tell the clerk?

a. Would you tell if you knew the cost of the item would be docked from the clerk's pay?

b. Would you tell if the clerk was your brother or sister?

3. More Questions: Some Moral Quandaries

Rudyard Kipling said, "Them that asks no questions isn't told a lie." That may not be the best advice in all circumstances. Here are some questions; to learn more about yourself, give a truthful response to them. Briefly jot down your answer in the space provided and then discuss your answers in small groups of four.

1. If a man fell over in the street in front of your school clutching his chest and gasping for air, what would you do?

2. Would you date someone of a different race? Why or why not?

3. At the lunch table some acquaintances begin to ridicule a friend of yours. Would you defend your friend even though you know they will pick on you next if you do?

4. A good friend of yours tells you that he or she is gay. What do you think you should do? What would you do?

5. If you discovered that your closest friend was pushing drugs at a local junior high, what would you do?

6. If an employer made inappropriate sexual advances to you at work, what would you do?

7. If a terrorist broke into your group and demanded that someone step forward to be executed or everyone would be killed, who would step forward? Would you?

8. Your sister needs a kidney transplant. If you donate your kidney, there is a small chance you'll die. Would you?

9. Do you use bad language? If so, is there anyone you would never use it in front of?

■ *discussion starters* ■

1. Are your answers typical of the group?
2. As a group, are you happy with the answers given?
3. Briefly discuss each situation from the point of view of the other person; for example, what if you were the man in situation 1? the person being ridiculed in situation 3? Can you imagine being the terrorist in situation 7?

---

4. Christian Values

Marshall Field lists twelve things he believes are important to remember:

1. The value of time.
2. The success of perseverance.
3. The pleasure of working.
4. The dignity of simplicity.
5. The worth of character.
6. The power of kindness.
7. The influence of example.
8. The obligation of duty.
9. The wisdom of economy.
10. The virtue of patience.
11. The improvement of talent.
12. The joy of origination.

■ *discuss* ■

Which of these do you think is most important?

Give examples from your own life that show several of these values to be true.

Jesus and the Christian community give us another list of key values that are the secret to joyful Christian living. Here is the list. Look through the gospels and find an example of each in Jesus' life. Then briefly describe a time when you exhibited the value in your own life.

The Values	In Jesus' life	In your life
Be just to all.		

The Values	In Jesus' life	In your life
Forgive as you have been forgiven.		
Care for those in need.		
Be honest in all dealings.		
Treat everyone as an individual.		
Be a person of peace.		
Respect life.		

CHOOSING

5. Movie Values

Use this analysis sheet to examine the values in a recent movie you have seen.

Select a movie you have seen in the past six months (and that you can remember well):

Briefly describe the main characters:

a.

b.

c.

Describe two scenes that raise moral issues. Discuss the stance the film takes toward these issues.

Scene   *Moral Stance*

1.

Scene
2.

Did you have positive or negative feelings toward the characters and the moral stances taken in the film? Explain how the film brought out these feelings in you.

List values in the film that could be considered Christian values. List values that go against Christian values.

Positive values	*Negative values*
1.	1.
2.	2.
3.	3.

Did this film support a positive or negative concept of the human person? Explain.

Did this film change your thinking about anything? If so, what? If not, why not?

■ *discussion* ■

1. Share your review of this movie with members of your group. Be prepared to discuss several of the values involved.
2. Would you say that most movies that appeal to teens today affect them negatively or positively? Explain by way of examples.
3. Think of the music used in a recent film you saw. Did the lyrics support positive or negative values? Explain.
4. What is your favorite song? What are the lyrics saying? Explain how the lyrics support or undermine traditional Christian values.
5. Videotape several rock videos. Analyze them in light of the questions given here.

---

6. Social Values

Societies promote certain values. Individuals may hold the values approved by their social group, or they may hold different ones. Small groups may have different values from the larger group they are part of. How do your values fit in with those approved by your society?

Part 1

Break into small groups of five or so. First, working individually, rank the values listed below. Give a #1 to the value you consider most important, a #2 to the second most important value and so on. Then compare and defend your rankings with other members of your group.

Individual		Majority
_____	equality between men and women	_____
_____	freedom to worship God as you wish	_____
_____	right to acquire property	_____
_____	justice in dealing with others	_____
_____	right of self-expression	_____
_____	tolerance for anyone who is different	_____
_____	economic security	_____
_____	freedom to travel	_____
_____	care for the poor and the suffering	_____
_____	discipline	_____

Part 2

1. In your small group discuss how you think the majority of people in our society would rank these same values. Mark these rankings in the column to the right.
2. Share your group's choices with those of other groups. Offer evidence to support your choices.

■ *discuss* ■

■ Compare your personal rankings with what your group believes the majority would choose. Are you a typical member of society or are you different?

■ Look at your top three rankings. How did you get these particular values? What seems to support and encourage them?

■ How might your values conflict with those of society? How might this cause problems for you in the future?

■ Which two values from the above list do you think are most consistent with the way Jesus lived his life? Give examples to support your conclusion.

7. Three Months to Live

We usually don't think of death in terms of the near future. We assume we have time to be better, to develop ourselves, to reach our goals. Setting a limit on life often brings our true values into sharper focus.

Step 1: Suppose you have a terminal illness. You have only three months more of life. The doctor says that you will feel little pain until the final week, so you can continue doing whatever you'd like to do. What are the ten things you would most like to do.

Rank

_____ 1. _____

_____ 2. _____

_____ 3. _____

_____ 4. _____

_____ 5. _____

_____ 6. _____

_____ 7. _____

_____ 8. _____

_____ 9. _____

_____ 10. _____

Step 2: Now rank your "last things to do" list in the order of importance to you with (1) most important, (2) second most important, etc.

Step 3: **Group Discussion** Compare your top three rankings with members of your group. Then broaden the discussion with the following questions:

1. Would you want to know when you were going to die? Why or why not?

2. What is the best way for a person your age to prepare for the death that will someday befall you?

3. If you were in a coma, would you want your family to use extraordinary means to keep you alive? Why or why not?

4. Do you believe in an afterlife? If so, does this belief affect the way you live your daily life? Explain.

8. Values and Your Philosophy of Life

Introduction: Our values often reflect how we view ourselves and other people. But sometimes our values are in conflict. For example, we may fiercely value our independence, yet we often go along with the group because we don't want to stand out.

Sticking to our true values often improves as we continue to develop a more consistent philosophy of life. As we grow in understanding how life, other people, God, and ourselves all fit together, we tend to be more steady in following through on what is most important to us.

Pause now to examine what is of most importance to you at this stage of your life's journey. What follows is a classic exercise in values clarification. Take no more than ten minutes to list the ten things you prize or cherish more than anything in the world.

—— 1. _____   —— 6. _____

—— 2. _____   —— 7. _____

—— 3. _____   —— 8. _____

—— 4. _____   —— 9. _____

—— 5. _____   —— 10. _____

Review your list and code your responses according to the following:

       P — choices that are persons

       * — items that are possessions

       $ — items that are financially valuable

       R — points that convey religious meaning (love, peace, justice)

       F — selections you share in common with your friends

■ *reflection* ■

In the space provided, write a short obituary announcing your death. Mention three values from the list above that describe what you believe to be important in your life.

———————————— DEATH NOTICE: ———————————

CHOOSING

9. What to Do?

Imagine that you have recently graduated from college. You are a sensitive, caring individual who has always wanted to help others.

You have been given the opportunity to do volunteer work as a lay person in a foreign country. You greatly admire the missionary order with whom you will work. In fact, one of its members inspired you to make a two-year commitment to this work. This person also told you that your unique ability to relate to young people will be a tremendous asset in spreading God's word. You really look forward to giving yourself to others before getting on with your career.

Unfortunately, the family doctor has told you that your father has an incurable form of cancer and may die within the next six months. But there is an equal chance that he will respond to treatment and survive for several years.

Your dad says he wants you to follow through on your commitment. Your mother thinks it is better for you to be available during your father's illness.

■ questions ■

1. Would it be wrong for you to leave home for the missions? Would it be wrong not to?

2. Do you have any other alternatives in this case? List some consequences of each of these alternatives.

3. Which has top priority—your family or those who desperately need you? Explain.

4. What would you do and why? What advice do you think Jesus would give you about this dilemma?

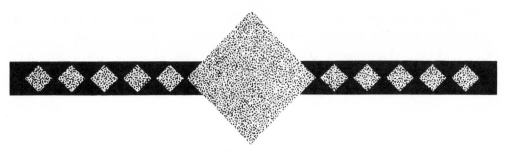

section two

Moral Decision-Making

Sometimes decisions in the area of morality are easy to make. The right thing to do is obvious; the wrong thing jumps out at us. However, many times our moral decisions require work on our part.

Several elements go into good decision-making. They include research, consultation, a period of incubation, prayer, and, ultimately, follow-through.

How do you know you are doing right? Fr. Gerard Sloyan in *How Do I Know I'm Doing Right?* (Dayton: Pflaum, 1976) suggests these kinds of questions:

- Do I have a pure intention in what I propose to do?

- Have I consulted the teachings of Jesus, the prophets, and St. Paul? Do I know what the Bible has to say about my issue?

- Is my action or my attitude loving?

- Have I consulted the church in forming my conscience: its official teachers—the pope and the bishops—and other holy and learned members? Have I considered my fellow believers and other people of good will?

- Do I follow the dictates of my conscience?

- Do I pray for God's guidance in all my decisions?

- Do I follow the great issues of our day (for example, peace, abortion, justice to the poor)?

- Do I acknowledge that I am a sinner and need God's forgiveness? Do I confess my sins, refusing to make excuses for them?
- Do I ask the Holy Spirit to form me into a person of love and strengthen me to resist negative peer pressure? Do I ask the Spirit to help me be the child of God that I truly am?

10. The STOP Sign Method for Making Moral Decisions

Case: You are at a friend's house. Several other friends are there also. Someone suggests pulling out a ouija board and playing around with it, asking questions and seeing what answers you come up with. You remember, however, that your religion teacher says the church condemns things like this because they are occult, superstitious practices that can lead one away from God to the realm of the devil. What would you do?

Here are the steps for using the STOP sign method of moral decision-making.

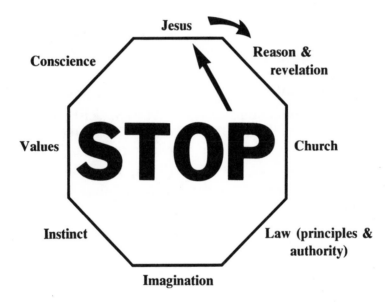

1. **Search** out the facts:
   What? Why? Who? When? Where? How?
   Remember these *principles:*
   - A good intention does not justify evil means to attain it.
   - If any part of the act is wrong (the action itself, the motive, or the circumstances), don't do it.
2. **Think** about:
   - the alternatives
   - the consequences
3. **Others**: consult and consider
   - talk to other people
   - how your action will affect them
4. **Pray**

JESUS: Does this action serve others? Is it loving?

REASON/REVELATION: Is this action human? What does the Bible say about it?

CHURCH: What does our church teach about this moral issue?

LAW: Consider the natural law as well as civil, church, and divine law.

IMAGINATION: Are there any creative ways to solve this problem?

INSTINCT: What do your "guts" tell you about this issue?

VALUES: List them and rank order them. Is the proposed act really worth it?

CONSCIENCE: Properly form it. Then follow it. **Act!**

---

11. Actor or Reactor

Jesus says "do unto others as you would have them do unto you." This command presumes that you will act on behalf of others, seek out their good, go out of your way to love them. Christian morality assumes that you will be an *actor* rather than a *reactor*. Reactors simply wait around for things to happen. They sit on the sidelines while life passes them by. They get involved only when they are forced by circumstances.

What about you? Are you a doer? Do you watch out for and respond to others? What would *you* do in the following situations?

1. A friend of yours habitually pokes fun at a classmate with a weight problem. What would you do?

2. You're downtown doing research at the library. A street person approaches you and asks for money for a cup of coffee. What would you do?

3. You have a seat on a crowded bus. An elderly person boards and has to stand. He or she catches your eye, and you know the person would like your seat. What would you do?

4. While walking through a drug store, you notice that a friend shoplifts a pack of gum. What would you do?

5. At Mass your pastor makes a general appeal to the youth of the parish for teachers' aides for the grade school parish religion program. You have the time to help out. What would you do?

6. The kids at your lunch table usually leave litter behind them when they leave. You never do, but it bothers you that they do. What would you do?

■ *discuss* ■

Compare answers. Then, for each of the items, discuss whether it would be moral or immoral for you to do nothing in each of the situations listed above.

CHOOSING

12. Alternatives and Consequences

When trying to make moral decisions, remember that you rarely have only *one* alternative. By using your imagination, by asking others for their advice, and by slowing down to consider the consequences of your proposed behavior, perhaps a new, more loving way to handle your problem will emerge.

Put yourself into the following situation. Consider what you should and would do in this case. But first, consider at least three alternatives and their consequences.

The Situation: **An Unfair Teacher**   A certain English teacher doesn't like you. He has no reason other than that he had your older brother in class. Your brother was something of a troublemaker and usually spoke his mind when he didn't like unfair policies. From day one of your course with this teacher, he has made snide, sarcastic remarks whenever he calls on you in class. He has embarrassed you several times, causing fellow students to laugh at you. Furthermore, you are convinced that he is grading your papers unfairly.

After a third poor grade you have a conference with the teacher. He defends his action and claims that *you* have an attitude problem. You do not make any progress talking to him. It is too late in the term to change teachers, and your counselor has advised you to "tough it out."

You are at your wit's end. What you really want to do is get even with this unfeeling, cruel teacher. Two of your friends say they will help you slash his tires. But you're not sure what you'll do.

What are your options? What are the consequences of each? What would you do?

Alternative 1:	Alternative 2:	Alternative 3:
Consequences:	*Consequences:*	*Consequences:*
1. _____	1. _____	1. _____
2. _____	2. _____	2. _____
3. _____	3. _____	3. _____

Your solution:

CHOOSING

13. Basis of Choice

Part 1: How we view a human person—our basic philosophy of life—is a strong influence on how we judge moral issues. Here are some statements that characterize some modern views of humanity. Judge what you believe about each using the following:

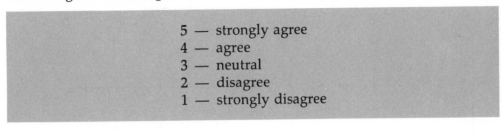

5 — strongly agree
4 — agree
3 — neutral
2 — disagree
1 — strongly disagree

_____ 1. Look out for Number One. I am Number One.

_____ 2. Get ahead of the pack using any means necessary.

_____ 3. Honesty is the best policy.

_____ 4. Forget rules; love is the measure of all things.

_____ 5. Live your life as Jesus would.

_____ 6. If it feels good, do it; if it feels bad, don't do it.

_____ 7. You won't go wrong if you follow the rules.

Part 2: Decide how you would act in the following situation if you held each of the positions described above. Briefly state why you would respond this way.

Case: You are in a shopping center parking lot. No one is around except an irritated young mother and her rambunctious toddler. Suddenly the mother loses control and starts beating her child. What would you do?

Action   Reason

1

2

3

4

5

6

7

14. Considering Others

None of our moral decisions is made in a vacuum. What we do or don't do affects others. We are members of a community of people with a network of intricate relationships. Intelligent, sensitive people consult others when making decisions. They calculate how their actions will affect others before they act.

How much should we depend on others in our decision-making?

> "To know the road ahead, ask those coming back."
> — Chinese proverb

> "I can give you a formula for failure: try to please everybody all the time."
> — Herbert Bayard Swope

That is, on the one hand, we must learn from others; on the other, we must follow our own best instincts.

Directions: Honestly decide what kind of person you are *and* what kind of person you would like to be. First, mark **X** on the spot on the scale where you think you are now. Second, mark * to indicate where you would like to be when you finish high school.

1. Do I ask advice before making a decision?

Always ask advice   **Always go it alone**

2. Do I think of others' feelings before acting?

Very considerate   **Inconsiderate**

3. Do I need other people to be happy?

Dependent   **Totally Independent**

4. Do I consider the consequences of my actions?

Always   **Never**

5. Do I cave in to peer pressure?

Never   **Always**

6. Do I consider the opinions of authority figures such as parents and teachers before acting?

Always   **Never**

15. The Discovery

This case, unfortunately, involves you.

You happen to be rummaging through your seventeen-year-old sister's belongings for the sweater she borrowed from you last week when you come across some birth control pills. The prescription is in her name. You know she has a steady boyfriend, but you never thought things had gone this far. What are you going to do? What should you do?

Directions: Think of three possible courses of action. List several consequences for each action.

Alternative #1: _____

Consequence a: _____

Consequence b: _____

Consequence c: _____

Alternative #2: _____

Consequence a: _____

Consequence b: _____

Consequence c: _____

Alternative #3: _____

Consequence a: _____

Consequence b: _____

Consequence c: _____

What would you probably do? Why?

16. Good Advice

When it comes to learning morality, we don't have to reinvent the wheel. Countless generations have come before us, made mistakes, lived their lives more or less successfully and left us much wonderful wisdom on how we should live.

William Safire and his brother Leonard compiled and edited two books entitled *Good Advice* (New York: Times Books, 1982) and *Words of Wisdom: More Good Advice* (New York: Simon and Schuster, 1989). There are some real nuggets of wisdom on how to live virtuous, happy lives among their thousands of entries. Here are some of them.

> *Directions:*   Read and reflect on the following quotations. Mark a plus (+) if you agree with the quote, a zero (0) if you disagree, and a question mark (?) if you are not sure. Answer the reflection questions that follow each quotation. Discuss your responses with other members of your group.

_____ *Ambition:*   "Keep away from people who try to belittle your ambitions. Small people always do that, but the really great make you feel that you, too, can become great" *(Mark Twain)*.

Who is the greatest person you associate with?

What makes this person great?

_____ **Success:** "Success is not so much achievement as achieving. Refuse to join the cautious crowd that plays not to lose; play to win" *(David Mahoney).*

What major goal are you striving for right now?

How do you play to win?

_____ **Contentment:** "Reflect on your present blessings, of which every man has many, not on your past misfortunes, of which all men have some" *(Charles Dickens).*

List three of your present blessings:

1) _____

2) _____

3) _____

_____ **Originality:** "If a man does not keep pace with his companions, perhaps it is because he hears a different drummer. Let him step to the music that he hears, however measured or far away" *(Henry David Thoreau).*

In what way are you different than any other person you know?

_____ *Patience:*   "Have patience with all things, but chiefly have patience with yourself. Do not lose courage in considering your own imperfections but instantly set about remedying them—every day begin the task anew" *(Saint Francis de Sales).*

In what aspect of your life do you need the most patience?

_____ *Example:*   "Be careful how you live. You may be the only Bible some person ever reads" *(William J. Toms).*

When was a time you gave bad example?

How did you feel afterward?

When was a time you gave good example?

How did you feel afterward?

_____ *Conscience:*   "The late Babe Didrikson Zaharias once disqualified herself from a tournament for having hit the wrong ball out of the rough. 'But nobody would have known,' a friend told her. 'I would've known,' Babe Didrikson Zaharias replied. Too many people in sports do not understand that now" *(Dave Anderson).*

Describe a time when you did the right thing even though no one else would have known if you had done wrong.

17. More Advice

Here is some more advice—both good and bad—on how you should live your life.

Bad Advice

Getting Ahead:

"Win anyway you can as long as you can get away with it. Nice guys finish last" *(Leo Durocher)*.

How to Live:

"Live fast, die young, have a beautiful corpse" *(motto of James Dean)*.

"Don't give a sucker an even break" *(Edward Francis Albee, popularized by W.C. Fields)*.

"Speak softly and carry a big stick; you will go far" *(Theodore Roosevelt)*.

"Don't rock the boat."

Good Advice

Discipline:

"No pain, no palm; no thorns, no throne; no gall, no glory; no cross, no crown" *(William Penn)*.

Ego:

"No one can make you feel inferior without your consent" *(Eleanor Roosevelt)*.

Evil:

"Keep five yards from a carriage, ten yards from a horse, and a hundred yards from an elephant; but the distance one should keep from a wicked man cannot be measured" *(Indian proverb)*.

Growth:

"Keep changing. When you're through changing, you're through" *(Bruce Barton)*.

Passion:

"Always refuse the advice that passion gives" (*English proverb*).

Riches:

"Who is rich? One who is happy with what he has" (*The Talmud,* **Pirkei Avot**, *4:1*).

Advice for a teenage daughter —five inexpensive beauty hints:

For lovely lips, speak words of kindness;
For lovely eyes, seek out the good in people;
For a slim figure, share your food with the hungry;
For beautiful hair, let a child run his fingers through it
  once a day;
And, for poise, walk with the knowledge that you will
  never walk alone.

Advice for a teenage son —five hints for strength of character:

For strong arms, exercise them by helping others;
For a handsome face, flash a smile at everyone you
  meet;
For a masculine voice, speak out on behalf of victims
  of injustice;
For virility, treat every female with utmost respect;
For heroic courage, make Jesus your best friend.

—Sam Levenson

CHOOSING

Now It Is Your Turn:　Here are five topics. Compose some advice you would give a younger brother or sister based on your own lived experience.

Happiness:

Judging others:

Honesty:

Commitment:

Success:

■ *discuss* ■

1. Share your advice with other members of your group.
2. Do you agree that all the items listed above under good and bad advice are categorized properly? If not, what would you change and why?
3. Discuss the meaning of each quotation. Give examples that might support or disprove them.

Moral Decision-Making

18. Humans: Good or Evil?

What is your view of human beings? Are people essentially good or evil? Think about the following statements. Then circle **Y** (yes) if you agree with the statement; **N** (no) if you disagree with the statement; or **?** if you don't know where you stand on this question.

I think that...

1. politicians are basically honest	Y	N	?
2. rapists and other violent criminals are probably just sick; they need psychiatric help	Y	N	?
3. good will eventually triumph over evil	Y	N	?
4. most people want to do the right thing	Y	N	?
5. honesty is the best policy	Y	N	?
6. virtue is its own reward	Y	N	?
7. people are basically greedy	Y	N	?
8. the world is too pleasure-oriented	Y	N	?
9. the arms race is proof that humanity is sick and in desperate need of a cure	Y	N	?
10. most people are lazy and take the easy way out	Y	N	?
11. people are like sheep; they are easily led and don't think for themselves	Y	N	?
12. people generally cheat if given the chance	Y	N	?

- Review your answers. In general do you have a positive or negative view of humanity?

- For those items you marked **Y** or **N**, offer some examples to support your view.

- Write a one-sentence description of how *you* view the human race:

19. Making a Decision

Please use the following worksheet to analyze a decision you are currently trying to make. Ask the Holy Spirit to enlighten you and lead you to a good decision and give you the courage to put it into action.

1. I am currently trying to decide:

2. Factors that are keeping me from deciding (or acting on my decision):

_____ I need some more information before deciding intelligently.

_____ It is not a pressing decision so I have been putting it off.

_____ I haven't looked at all the alternatives open to me.

_____ I am afraid of the price I might have to pay if I follow through on this decision.

_____ I am afraid of what others might think.

Some other factors that are holding me back:

3. Three people who could help me get off dead center on this decision are:

Person: *How he/she could help*

_____   _____

_____   _____

_____   _____

4. What are the two worst things that could happen as a result of this decision?

a. _____   b. _____

5. What are the two best things that could happen as a result of this decision?

a. _____   b. _____

6. Pretend that you went to talk to Jesus about your decision. Picture him sitting next to you while you talk out your various options. What advice would he give you?

7. What three precise steps must you take right now to work out this decision?

a. _____

b. _____

c. _____

8. What must you do during the coming week to move toward your goal? Fill in the calendar of what you must do and when you will do it:

monday _____

tuesday _____

wednesday _____

thursday _____

friday _____

saturday/sunday _____

9. Having gone through this exercise, what do you think at this very early stage about what you will do?

Optional: If you wish, share and discuss what you wrote with a close friend. Ask this person to check back with you in a week's time to see how you are progressing.

CHOOSING

20. Moral Decision-Making

Psychologist Lawrence Kohlberg studied moral decision-making. In his view there are six major stages of moral reasoning. We move to a higher stage when people who reason at a stage above ours challenge our thinking. Here is a thumbnail sketch of Kohlberg's six stages with an example for each.

Levels	Stages	Examples
Preconventional— Focus on myself (*Comment*: Most children reason on this level.)	*Stage 1:* **Punishment or Obedience** I submit to authority figures because of the physical consequences for me if I don't.	First-grader Jimmy doesn't take Billy's crayons because the teacher will punish him if he does.
	Stage 2: **Personal Usefulness** Something is right if I get something out of it.	Fifth-grader Sue brings in $5 for the missions because her teacher said she wouldn't have any homework for a week if she did.
Conventional — Focus on the group (*Comment*: Kohlberg claims that most people reason on this level.)	*Stage 3:* **Good Boy or Girl** I do something to get the approval and praise of others. I conform to group standards of what is right or wrong.	Ninth-grader Jack drinks beer at the party because everyone else is doing it.
	Stage 4: **Law and Order** I obey the rules of the system to maintain right order. Right behavior consists in doing my duty.	Dan obeys the traffic laws for the good of society. He says that if people didn't obey the laws, there would be chaos on our highways.

**Postconventional —
Focus on principles**

Stage 5: **Social Contract**
Right action flows from general principles agreed on in a society and on personal values. I should work to change a law if it will help make society more self-respecting.

Sally, the mother of four children, is active in the pro-life movement. She writes letters to state legislators petitioning them to outlaw capital punishment.

Stage 6: **Personal Conscience**
I make my decisions based on ethical principles that apply to all persons everywhere — justice, equality, the dignity of every human life.

Mother Teresa of Calcutta takes a dying leper into her arms. She says she is ministering to Jesus Christ.

■ *exercise* ■

Here are four short situations. Judge which stage a person is at in his or her moral reasoning. Give a reason for your choice. Then discuss what you would do in a similar situation and why.

_____ 1. Bob dented the family car in the parking lot last night. He decides to tell his father the truth, accept the consequences, and hope that his dad will let him use the car next weekend.

_____ 2. As a last resort Tim asks Mary to the homecoming dance. Mary says yes. A week later Tim breaks the date with Mary to ask Jennifer, the person he really wanted to ask in the first place. He was afraid Jennifer wouldn't go with him, but Tim's friend Gary found out that Jennifer likes Tim.

_____ 3. Marcia always makes sure she cleans up after herself and at least one other person in the school cafeteria. Her reason? It's her school, and she takes pride in it.

_____ 4. The English teacher has assigned a difficult Dickens novel. She is asking for a five-page paper and will give four quizzes on the novel. Many of Joyce's classmates have decided to take a shortcut—buy and read "notes" on the novel. Joyce refuses to take the easy way out because she will only be cheating herself.

21. Whom to Believe?

Many people and institutions in society are competing for your allegiance. Their reasons vary. Some may want you to buy something—a pair of jeans, a CD, a skin-care product. Others may promise you something to get your vote. Some may want you to accept their philosophy of life regardless of what it is—hedonism, materialism, consumerism. Still others genuinely care about you and want to inform you about an idea for your own good: Don't do drugs! Don't smoke! Buckle your seat belt!

Analyze how people try to win you over to their point of view. They often use certain techniques of persuasion that have been proven effective in convincing people of something. Some of these are good, honest, and straightforward. Others are more subtle and duplicitous. As a Christian, you need to be your own person, to figure out for yourself what is true and for your true good. Thus, you need to think clearly and recognize the various techniques people use to win you over.

Here is a list of persuasive techniques with a short description of each. Following are some examples. Match the examples with the techniques.

Prejudice—an unwillingness to examine the evidence on behalf of a person or thing because of a preconceived opinion.

Oversimplification—an explanation of a complex event by only one or two possible causes when many causes are equally plausible.

Appearance—acceptance or rejection of a thing or person based solely on appearances without any consideration that the appearance might be deceptive.

Popularity—promotion of an idea or product based on large numbers of people who approve it.

Slogans—catchy phrases designed to side-step thought and promote action in favor of a slogan-maker's product or belief.

Personal attack—a direct attack on the person holding a particular point of view rather than on the point of view itself.

Rationalization—reasons used to justify an action that was really based on other grounds.

Endorsement—an appeal based on our respect for the person who promotes the product or belief.

Example	*Technique*

1. Pro-lifers are sexually repressed. They like forcing their views on others. _____

2. Legalize cocaine and the crime problem would go away. _____

3. Too many of our tax dollars go to the poor. Most are welfare cheats anyhow and are too lazy to get a job. _____

4. "Live a little." (Words to accompany a beer commercial.) _____

5. "Don't be caught without a pair of our jeans. They're the 'in' thing." _____

6. "If my parents weren't so strict, I wouldn't have to sneak around." _____

7. "Why listen to her? She's only a nun and doesn't know anything about life anyhow." _____

8. "They look like they're having a lot of fun. What could possibly be wrong about joining in?" _____

Project: Examine some magazines, newspapers, and the television to find advertisements that exhibit several of the appeals described above.

Then, analyze a recent editorial intended to promote a certain position on a controversial topic. Note any techniques of persuasion used.

▪ *discuss* ▪

1. Do you feel manipulated by the media? For example, listen to the ads and announcements of your favorite radio station. What are some of the values being sold along with the products? Are you forced to compare yourself with others? Explain.

2. Discuss some examples from the media that sell the idea of immediate gratification. What are some dangers of immediate self-indulgence to Christian moral living?

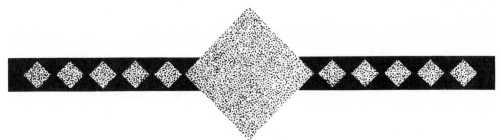

section three

Jesus

All of us are familiar with the following cliché: Imitation is the highest form of flattery. When we really like someone—a teacher, a parent, a sports figure—we often select some aspect of his or her life and set out to imitate it, either consciously or unconsciously.

A good way to grow in the Christian life is to imitate our Christian heroes, courageous men and women who lived or live heroic lives of love. However, no person is worth studying more carefully than Jesus, who said:

"I am the Way; I am Truth and Life.
No one can come to the Father except through me.
If you know me, you will know my Father too.

"If you love me you will keep my commandments"
(Jn 14:6,15).

The following exercises help us get in touch with Jesus, who shows us the way to live truly human, upright, loving lives of service.

22. The Bible and Morality

The Bible is a rich source of moral knowledge. Listed below are some moral issues. Please look up the Bible references given and then briefly summarize what the Bible teaches about this issue.

Moral Issue	Bible References	Summary
Divorce	Mk 10:1-2	_____
	Lk 16:18	_____
	Mt 5:31-32	_____
	Mt 19:1-9, 23-26	_____
Justice	Lv 19:9-10	_____
	Ps 146:5-8	_____
	Am 5:21-24	_____
	Lk 12:32-48	_____
	Jas 2:14-17, 26	_____
Drunkenness	Prv 23:31	_____
	Eph 5:18	_____
Lying	Dt 5:20	_____
	Eph 4:24-25	_____

Obedience	Lv 19:3	_____
	Sir 3:1-16	_____
	Mk 7:9-13	_____
Sexual morality	Col 3:5, 6	_____
	1 Cor 3:16	_____
	Lv 18:22	_____
	Mt 5:32	_____

■ *discussion* ■

1. Are these teachings as relevant today as in biblical times? Explain.
2. What role should moral teachings from the Bible play in the formation of our consciences?
3. Can a person justifiably act contrary to an *explicit* moral teaching from the Bible? Why or why not? Give examples.

23. The Golden Rule

Many religions claim that love is a basic force in making moral decisions. The following statements assume that we have a healthy love and respect for ourselves:

Buddhism:	"Hurt not others with that which pains thyself" (fifth century B.C.).
Confucianism:	"What you don't want done to yourself, don't do to others" (sixth century B.C.).
Zoroastrianism:	"Do not do unto others all that which is not well for oneself" (fifth century B.C.).
Judaism:	"What is hateful to yourself, don't do to your fellow man" (Rabbi Hillel, first century B.C.).
Christianity:	"Do unto others as you would have them do unto you" (Jesus, first century).

■ *reflection* ■

1. How do *you* define love?

2. Give two examples of love you witnessed today:

a.

b.

3. What is the essential difference between the teaching of Jesus and the other teachings listed above?

Case: You suspect that a friend is using drugs. You've tried talking to her but have had no luck. You really like your friend and don't want to get her into any trouble. What should you do?

1. What is most loving to do in this case?

2. What advice might each of the religions quoted above give?

3. What would you do? What should you do?

24. Jesus and Some Moral Issues

Jesus provides us with a rich source of guidance on living the moral life. He taught the kind of attitudes we should have to respond lovingly to God and others. Although Jesus did not offer specific teachings on many moral issues, he did address certain controversial topics in morality, topics that are as relevant today as they were in his lifetime.

Check these passages to see what Jesus said about the following topics:

Topic	Passage	Short Summary of Jesus' Teaching
Adultery	Mt 5:27-30	
Violence	Mt 5:38-42	
Worry	Mt 7:25-34	
Wealth	Mk 10:23-27	
Taxes	Lk 20:20-26	
Kindness	Mk 12:41-44	
Integrity	Lk 6:29-45	
Forgiveness	Jn 8:1-11	

■ discuss ■

List on a separate sheet of paper the ten worst worries of teens. Then discuss why these worries are counterproductive. Give an antidote for each of these worries.

25. Jesus Teaches

Here are some key, life-giving sayings of Jesus Christ. They contain the good news of God's love and some commands on how we should live our lives. Rate your attitude to them by using the following scale.

1 — This saying has tremendous meaning for me and I agree with it.

2 — I want to believe this, and I want to make sense out of it.

3 — I am not sure if I believe this or not.

4 — I don't understand this, or if I do understand it, I can't agree with it.

_____ "In truth I tell you, in so far as you did this to one of the least of these brothers of mine, you did it to me" (Mt 25:40).

_____ "So always treat others as you would like them to treat you; that is the Law and the Prophets" (Mt 7:12).

_____ "Be compassionate just as your Father is compassionate. Do not judge, and you will not be judged; do not condemn, and you will not be condemned; forgive, and you will be forgiven" (Lk 6:36-37).

_____ "Ask, and it will be given to you; search, and you will find; knock and the door will be opened to you" (Lk 11:9).

_____ "Anyone who wants to become great among you must be your servant" (Mk 10:43).

_____ "I am the light of the world; anyone who follows me will not be walking in the dark but will have the light of life" (Jn 8:12).

■ *reflection* ■

1. Who are the "least of these" you meet each day?

   What can you do for them?

2. Who needs your forgiveness?

3. What is your greatest need?

   Will you ask the Lord to fulfill it?

4. List two ways you can serve others *right now*:

a.

b.

26. Money and You

What is of value to us colors how we make decisions in our lives. For example, we live in a society that often judges us by how much money we have. There is a danger that we might think what we have determines how valuable we are as people. Henry Fielding warned: "Make money your god and it will plague you like the devil."

> What is your reaction to the following statements? Mark **SA** for "strongly agree"; **A** for "agree"; **D** for "disagree"; and **SD** for "strongly disagree."

_____ 1. "The love of money is the root of all evil."

_____ 2. "Take the money and run" (American saying).

_____ 3. "Money can't buy happiness."

_____ 4. "Never esteem a man or thyself the more for money, nor condemn him for want of it" (English proverb).

_____ 5. "If you don't watch out for yourself, no one else will."

_____ 6. "The rich get richer and the poor get poorer."

_____ 7. "Money isn't everything; money is the only thing."

■ discuss ■

Share your responses and give reasons for your choices.

What did Jesus say? Christians need to consult the teachings of Jesus when they form their attitudes toward money. Here are several things Jesus taught about money. Read them and then discuss the questions that follow.

- "No servant can be the slave of two masters: he will either hate the first and love the second, or be attached to the first and despise the second. You cannot be the slave of both God and money" (Lk 16:13).

- "Yes, I tell you again, it is easier for a camel to pass through the eye of a needle than for someone rich to enter the kingdom of Heaven" (Mt 19:24).

- "Watch, and be on guard against avarice of any kind, for life does not consist in possessions, even when someone has more than he needs" (Lk 12:15).

- "If you wish to be perfect, go and sell your possessions and give the money to the poor, and you will have treasure in heaven; then come, follow me" (Mt 19:21).

- "How blessed are the poor in spirit: the kingdom of Heaven is theirs" (Mt 5:3).

■ discussion ■

1. Based on the quotations given above, why does the Lord warn us against riches? Give some examples of how inordinate wealth can enslave a person.

2. What does it mean to be rich? to be poor?

3. What does it mean to be "poor in spirit"?

4. How do you know if money is beginning to control your life? What can you do about it?

5. Could you drop everything and follow Jesus? Explain. Does Jesus call everyone to do this?

6. As a group, construct a list of five rules people should observe if they are wealthy.

CHOOSING

27. Self-Evaluation on Prayer

Jesus teaches us this profound truth:

"Ask, and it will be given to you; search, and you will find; knock, and the door will be opened to you. Everyone who asks receives; everyone who searches finds; everyone who knocks will have the door opened. Is there anyone among you who would hand his son a stone when he asked for bread? Or would hand him a snake when he asked for a fish? If you, then, evil as you are, know how to give your children what is good, how much more will your Father in heaven give good things to those who ask him!" (Mt 7:7-11).

Prayer is indispensable for the Christian who desires to live a moral life. But what is prayer? Traditionally, we define prayer as the raising of our minds and hearts to God in Adoration, Contrition, Thanksgiving, and Supplication. (Note the anagram, ACTS.) In other words, in prayer, we praise God, express sorrow for sins, express our gratitude for the many gifts God has given us, and ask God to respond to our needs.

Another way to look at prayer is as a loving conversation with the Lord which involves both talking and listening. Like any intimate conversation with a friend, prayer requires faith and trust, the belief that our Lord indeed loves us and wants only what is good for us.

There are many ways to pray — alone, with others, meditatively, vocally, using formal prayers, using your own words, and the like. Here are some ways that Christians consider to be potentially meaningful prayer experiences. Indicate how frequently you engage in each of them using the following rating system:

VF — very frequently
S — sometimes
F — frequently
N — never

_____ 1. Asking God to cure sick friends and relatives.

_____ 2. Asking God for help in studies or athletic endeavors.

_____ 3. Participating in the Mass.

_____ 4. Reading the Bible.

_____ 5. Asking for God's help to resist temptation.

_____ 6. Thinking about the life and example of Jesus.

_____ 7. Thanking God for the beautiful things in creation.

_____ 8. Reciting the rosary.

_____ 9. Saying grace before and after meals.

_____ 10. Asking God for forgiveness after doing something wrong.

_____ 11. Realizing that God is present in all creation—including you.

_____ 12. Examining your conscience each night before going to sleep.

_____ 13. Reflecting on the good things that you have and thanking God for them.

_____ 14. Talking to God informally as a friend.

_____ 15. Reading spiritual books.

_____ 16. Trying to figure out, with God's help, why certain people have come into your life and why certain things have happened the way they did.

_____ 17. Reciting formal prayers like the Our Father.

_____ 18. Spending quiet time in a chapel or church.

_____ 19. Asking for the Lord's help when trying to make a decision.

_____ 20. Consciously trying to see God in other people.

■ *reflection* ■

What is your favorite way to pray? Describe a time it has helped you.

28. The Sermon on the Mount

The Sermon on the Mount (Mt 5—7) summarizes the ethical code of Jesus. Any Christian wanting to act morally must form his or her conscience in light of it. Please read the sermon, then turn to the following exercise. Place an **X** in the appropriate column to indicate whether you think the action is *morally right*, *morally wrong*, or *not a moral issue*. Then go back over the items you marked as morally wrong and rank order them from the worst moral issue (1), the next most serious moral issue (2), etc.

Rank	Item	Right	Wrong	No Issue
_____	1. Holding a grudge against someone			
_____	2. Failing to witness to the gospel when the opportunity presents itself			
_____	3. Holding a grudge against someone who hurt you			
_____	4. Taking an oath in court			
_____	5. Liking your friends more than strangers			
_____	6. Giving money to the poor with the intention that someone will notice your generosity			
_____	7. Failing to fast during the Lenten season			
_____	8. Earning money and saving it for some future purchase			
_____	9. Worrying about where you might go to college			
_____	10. Finding fault with someone's annoying habits			
_____	11. Not saying night prayers			
_____	12. Performing one's duties—like studies—haphazardly			

■ *discuss* ■

What is the most serious moral demand of the Sermon on the Mount?

29. The Sermon on the Mount: The Beatitudes

How blessed are the poor in spirit:
the kingdom of Heaven is theirs.
Blessed are *the gentle:*
they shall have the earth as inheritance.
Blessed are those who mourn:
they shall be comforted.
Blessed are those who hunger and thirst for uprightness:
they shall have their fill.
Blessed are the merciful:
they shall have mercy shown them.
Blessed are the pure in heart:
they shall see God.
Blessed are the peacemakers:
they shall be recognized as children of God.
Blessed are those who are persecuted in the cause of
uprightness:
the kingdom of Heaven is theirs.

Blessed are you when people abuse you and per-
secute you and speak all kinds of calumny against you
falsely on my account. Rejoice and be glad, for your
reward will be great in heaven; this is how they persecuted the prophets before you" (Mt 5:3-12).

Poor in spirit: _____ Do I accept that God is the source of everything in my life?

Gentle: _____ Am I truly a gentle person?

Mourn: _____ When I see unfairness do I do something about it?

Uprightness: _____ Do I really want to be a good person?

Merciful: _____ Do I forgive others when they hurt me?

Pure in heart: _____ Am I an authentic person, one who can be trusted?

Peacemaker: _____ When confronted with conflict, am I part of the solution rather than part of the problem?

Persecuted: _____ If it were a crime to be a Christian, would there be enough evidence to convict me?

Complete this new beatitude:

"How blessed am I when _____ ."

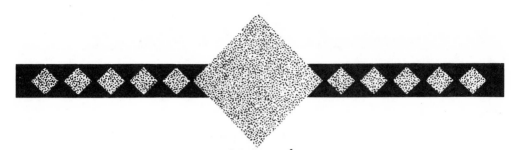

section four

Principles

Good moral principles and laws serve an important function in the moral life. They represent the accumulated wisdom of those who have come before us. They embody experience and outline the boundaries of moral behavior.

Catholic moral reflection has always recognized the importance of law and principles, the objective norm of morality. At their best, they serve as guiding beacons to ethical behavior.

The Ten Commandments and the golden rule are excellent summaries of divine law. Other principles, like philosopher Immanuel Kant's ethical guide—"So act that your principle of action might safely be made a law for the whole world"—embody norms that wise and good men and women have used to guide their lives through the centuries.

Good law and practical principles guarantee human freedom; they do not extinguish it. Exercising one's freedom responsibly while taking into consideration the guidance of good principles is an important dimension of mature growth in the moral life.

30. Commandments for Parents and Teens

Gather into small groups of three or so. Compose a list of ten commandments for parents. Then compose another list of ten commandments for teens. Try to state principles that will help adults and teens live happy, productive, responsible lives.

Here are some quotes that might stimulate your thinking:

Principles for Living:

1. "This above all; to thine own self be true" (Polonius in Shakespeare's *Hamlet*).

2. "Judge not lest you be judged" (Jesus of Nazareth).

3. "Fall seven times, stand up eight" (Japanese proverb).

4. "Less is more. God is in the details" (Miles van der Rohe).

5. "So live that you wouldn't be ashamed to sell the family parrot to the town gossip" (Will Rogers).

6. "If you start to take Vienna, take Vienna" (Napoleon Bonaparte).

7. "If you can't win, make the fellow ahead of you break the record" (Anonymous).

8. "Don't worry about anything; instead, pray about everything; tell God your needs and don't forget to thank him for his answers" (St. Paul, Phil 4:6, *TLB*).

9. "Don't just sit there, do something" (Popular American saying).

10. "Don't just do something, sit there" (Thich Nhat Hanh on the valuable role of meditation in our lives).

Parent Commandments

1: _____

2: _____

CHOOSING

3: _____

4: _____

5: _____

6: _____

7: _____

8: _____

9: _____

#10: _____

Teen Commandments

1: _____

2: _____

3: _____

4: _____

5: _____

6: _____

7: _____

8: _____

9: _____

#10: _____

▪ *discussion* ▪

What are the major similarities and differences between the two groups? Discuss three principles you believe both parents and teens should strongly adhere to.

31. Exception to the Rule?

Rules are made to be broken... or are they? Rules help guide right behavior. Allow too many exceptions and you might be asking for trouble. Consider this case.

Fr. Bob Manners is principal of St. John Berchmans High School, an all-male, college-prep Catholic school. He runs an excellent school, which is big on academics, sports, and discipline. Some parents make many sacrifices to send their sons there, and most of the students take great pride in their school. The sense of being a religious school is strong. There is an active retreat program at St. John's, and every senior is expected to make a three-day retreat away from school. Many creative options are given the students, and most students profit from this experience to draw closer to the Lord.

Fr. Bob has a very strict policy, though, of expelling from the school any senior caught doing drugs or drinking alcohol on the retreat. In a recent year there was an ugly incident. Some students were involved in an alcohol-related accident driving home from the retreat. A small child was killed at a crosswalk. Since then, Fr. Bob has taken this extreme measure of mandatory expulsion for any student caught drinking on retreats. Students and parents both understand and agree to this policy before being admitted to the school. The rule is reviewed before students embark on the retreat.

This year Gary Farmer, son of a multi-millionaire, was caught drinking in his room after the second night of the retreat. This is the first time in his high school career that Gary has been caught doing anything wrong, but he clearly violated school policy. He can't imagine the principal taking action in his case, though. He knows Fr. Bob has a real dilemma. Though his policy states that Gary should be kicked out of the school, Gary's father said if this action is taken, he will not follow through on a half-million dollar pledge for the newly-planned laboratory complex for both art and science classes. Without Mr. Farmer's donation, the school will not be able to have a much needed facility. What should Fr. Bob do?

■ *discussion* ■

1. Should Fr. Bob make an exception? What would be some conse-quences if he decided this either way? What is the just thing to do in this case?

2. Is the original rule a good rule? Why or why not?

3. How should schools control the consumption of alcohol at school-related events? Is this a problem in your school?

4. Do authority figures in your school have a double standard when doling out punishment to students? Explain with examples.

32. Freedom to Choose

Responsible decision-making implies the presence of two kinds of freedom. *External* freedom enables us to act without undue restraint or control of another. *Internal* freedom, on the other hand, comes from within. It is the state of mind and spirit which enables us to achieve our full human potential.

Here are three situations where external freedom is present. Thus, the condition is present where you can choose to act in a way that will enable you to grow as a human person, a child of God with dignity. How would you exercise your freedom?

1. Your father and mother have gone out of town on a business trip. Your brothers and sisters are staying with relatives. You will remain alone in the house. Your parents have instructed you not to have any friends over. What would you do?

2. You work as a waitress in an ice cream shop. The store policy is that employees are allowed one sundae or its equivalent every night they work. They may not give free ice cream treats to friends. However, it is impossible for the owner to monitor his employees since he is not there most of the time. Would you keep his policy?

3. The night before an important game against a rival school, your best friend asks you to go to a concert with her. Your coach told you to be in bed by 9 p.m. so you'd have plenty of rest for the contest. You can't possibly be home from the concert until after midnight. And there would still be homework to do. What would you do?

■ *discuss* ■

1. Would it be morally wrong for you to go against the wishes of any of the authority figures in the various stories? Explain.
2. What principles of good behavior are at stake in each of the cases?

33. Law and Morality

Good law is like the foul line in baseball or the boundary lines on a football field. These lines show where the game should be played. Once the ball goes outside the lines the ball is dead and play must start over again.

St. Thomas Aquinas taught that good law is (1) reasonable, (2) issued by proper authority, (3) directed at the common good, and (4) advertised in a way that people know about it. Good law is an *objective measure* against which we can assess our behavior. It usually points out the minimum acceptable behavior for harmonious human living. If we violate the law, we are *usually* "out of bounds" in the moral life, too.

Here is a list of laws various societies have promulgated (issued) over the years. Decide if the law is good (**G**) or bad (**B**).

_____ 1. The speed limit for school zones is 20 mph.

_____ 2. All eighteen-year-old males must register for the draft.

_____ 3. Catholics must receive the eucharist at least once a year, during the Easter season (from the first Sunday of Lent through Trinity Sunday).

_____ 4. No alcoholic beverages may be sold to or consumed by anyone under the age of eighteen years.

_____ 5. There should be mandatory, random testing for drug use among air traffic controllers.

_____ 6. Everyone earning over $60,000 is liable to a 30 percent income tax.

_____ 7. Same-sex marriages are not recognized by the law.

_____ 8. Smoking in public places is strictly prohibited.

_____ 9. It is a felony subject to a heavy fine and imprisonment to burn the American flag.

▪ discuss ▪

1. If you decided a particular law was good, discuss how it is reasonable and protects the common good.

2. How are each of these laws designed to help people live happy, productive lives. Are they effective?

3. Analyze ten school rules (laws). Discuss why they are good or bad. How might they help school life?

34. Moral Principles

An important principle in making moral decisions is to choose the human thing to do. We rarely go wrong when we act in accord with our true nature. Chapter 1 of the Second Vatican Council's document *The Pastoral Constitution on the Church in the Modern World* reminds us that humans:

- have basic dignity which flows from their being created in God's image;
- are body-persons who are related to others in community;
- are spiritual beings with souls which means that we can think, make free choices, and love;
- are fundamentally good, but are prone to evil; we are indeed capable of sinning, but God will always love us;
- have a conscience—a judgment of right and wrong—which helps us make decisions to respond in a moral way to God and others;
- are children of God, brothers and sisters to each other, who must care for the welfare of others.

Which of the following are wrong because they deny what it means to be God's special creature? Check off any items you believe are inhuman. Discuss the reasons for your choices. Add three items to this list of actions and attitudes. Share these with members of your group.

_____ lying to avoid embarrassment

_____ telling racial jokes

_____ laughing at racial jokes

_____ insulting a teacher behind her back

_____ riding in a car without wearing a seat belt

_____ directing vulgar language to an umpire who made a bad call

_____ governments paying farmers to plow under surplus crops

_____ revealing someone's secrets

_____ consistently not studying

_____ refusing to vote

_____ testing nuclear weapons

_____ possessing nuclear weapons

_____ incest

Your three:

1.

2.

3.

35. Principle of Double Effect

Catholic moral theology has developed several important moral principles; for example, a good end does not justify using evil means to attain it. In other words you may not do an evil action to attain a good outcome. Good intentions do not justify bad behavior.

But what about the case where your action, though good or neutral in and of itself, results in *two* simultaneous effects: one good, the other evil. Are you permitted to engage in this action? Under certain conditions you are. This is the so-called principle of double effect.

Double effect really means side effect. The principle of double effect allows bad effects that result from your good actions if there is proportionate reason for your action. Let's take an example. Grandmother is terminally ill with cancer and is suffering excruciating pain. Would the doctors be justified in using large quantities of pain-killing drugs, even though these drugs might seriously damage Grandma's respiration? The answer is yes, *if*:

1. The action that causes the two effects is not evil itself.

2. The intention of the agent is good. What is willed is the good effect (lessening the pain). Even though the evil effect is foreseen (damage to the respiratory system), it is not desired.

3. The good effect cannot be obtained by means of the evil effect.

4. The good effect must be sufficiently desirable for allowing the evil effect to take place. In other words, there must be a proportionately grave reason for allowing the evil to occur.

Given these principles, discuss the proper course of action in the following cases. Which principles apply?

Case 1:   A woman is pregnant. She also has cancer of the uterus, which threatens her life. Can the doctors remove her womb, even though the operation will result in the death of the child within it?

Case 2:   A parent has a healthy kidney removed so that it can be given to her child. The child would die without a new kidney.

Case 3:   A woman has an abortion to protect her reputation.

Case 4:   A student loses a night of sleep studying for a physics exam.

Case 5:   The military bombs a munitions factory, knowing that there is a risk to innocent people who live nearby.

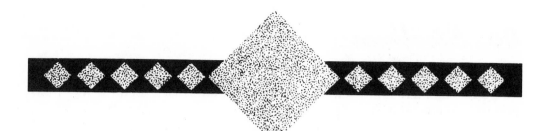

section five

Life and Death Issues

Life is God's most precious gift to us. We must care for it, cherish and nourish it, and share it with others. To be Christian means to be pro-life.

However, today there are many assaults on human life and the dignity of human persons. Abortion, suicide, drug addiction, euthanasia, the arms race, crippling poverty, malnutrition and starvation, environmental deterioration, complex ethical cases in medicine . . . the list is endless.

Here are some cases that you read about. Others are the result of an increasingly complex technology. Still others confront us as fellow travelers on the spaceship earth.

36. Bioethics

Bioethics, literally, the ethics of life, is "the study of the ethical and moral questions involved in the application of new biological and medical findings." Such questions arise in the fields of genetic engineering, neurobiology, and drug research, among others. This is a complex, but very important, branch of morality. As scientific knowledge and experimentation increase, more and more life issues are raised. Christians must always think about these issues in terms of a human, loving response.

Discussion about these issues for Catholics presumes research and reflection. However, here are several principles that must govern all debates about bioethical issues.

Principle 1: God is the author of life. Humans are the image of God. Thus, human life has profound dignity. It is sacred and deserves respect.

Principle 2: We can't do something evil to obtain a good end. Good intentions do not justify evil actions.

Principle 3: Sometimes neutral actions result in both good and bad effects. Given certain conditions, we may engage in such neutral actions. These conditions include:
> a. The action must be good or neutral.
> b. The good can't be obtained by means of the evil.
> c. The evil effects must not be intended, only permitted.
> d. There must be sufficient reason for engaging in the action.
> e. The action must be the last resort.

Principle 4: Sometimes called the principle of totality, this means that a part exists for the good of the whole. Thus, as a last resort, a person may dispose of a diseased body part in order to preserve his or her life.

Principle 5: A person must use ordinary means to preserve his or her life. Ordinary means are medicines, treatments, and operations that offer a reasonable benefit and that can be obtained and used without excessive pain, expense, or inconvenience. On the other hand, a person is not ethically required to use extraordinary means to preserve life.

Principle 6: Every human life is valuable—from the moment of conception to the moment of death. Everyone has the right to the minimal medical care required to live a happy, productive, healthy life.

Principle 7: Jesus continues to teach through his church. In thinking through biomedical issues, Catholics must consult the teaching of the church—both magisterial teaching and theological reflection.

Biomedical Issues: With the principles of bioethical decisions in hand, discuss the rightness or wrongness of the following biomedical issues:

1. *Genetic engineering:*

_____ a. of plants like corn to make it resistant to frost

_____ b. of humans to help cure diseases like sickle cell anemia

_____ c. of microbial pesticides

_____ d. of viruses that lead to the creation of vaccines which might cure AIDS or cancer

■ *questions* ■

1. What harmful effects might result from altering the natural order of evolution?
2. Is it wrong to try to create a "perfect" human being? If genetic engineers could prolong the human lifespan to 200 years, would this be playing God?
3. Should genetic engineering be controlled? How?

2. *Reproductive technology:*

_____ a. artificial insemination by a donor

_____ b. artificial insemination by a husband

_____ c. in vitro fertilization (fertilization of an ovum by a sperm outside the uterus)

_____ d. surrogate motherhood (a person who for financial reasons or compassionate motives agrees to bear a child for another)

_____ e. experimentation on embryos (prefetal human life up to the third month of conception)

■ *questions* ■

1. Does a married couple have a *right* to have children?
2. In what way may each of the cases listed above be considered "unnatural"?
3. Is surrogate motherhood another name for "baby buying"?
4. What consequences might these various technologies have for the way we view the family? motherhood? fatherhood?
5. Should embryos have the protection of law?

3. *Organ transplants:*

_____ a. hearts _____   livers _____   kidneys _____
            corneas _____   pancreas _____   lungs _____

_____ b. selling body parts for money (for example, a kidney)

_____ c. artificial hearts

■ *questions* ■

1. Can organ transplants lead to lack of respect for the dead?

2. Have you signed a driver's license instructing that your organs be donated should you die in a car accident? Why or why not?

3. Could widespread use of organ transplantation lead to euthanasia?

4. Does organ transplantation favor the rich over the poor? Does it tend to dehumanize people, making them more like pieces of property rather than humans?

5. Is the expense of developing organ transplant technology a wise use of limited medical resources?

6. Should parents have the right to donate a non-life-threatening organ of a minor child to his or her sibling without the child's consent?

4. *Cryogenics* (science of low-temperature phenomena):

_____ a. preserving a diseased body until some future time when a cure is found

_____ b. preserving an aged body until life-prolongation technologies have been perfected

■ *questions* ■

1. Is this type of technology a denial of the resurrection of the body?

2. Should science be permitted to do whatever it can do in biomedical research? Why or why not?

37. Health-Care Ethics: Survey and Research

Part 1: **Directions**: Here is a list of pressing health-care concerns. Rank them from the most important (**1**) to the least important (**10**). Share your rankings and your reasons for choosing the way you did.

_____ significantly raising the salaries of nurses

_____ health-care programs designed to insure minimal health maintenance for *all* citizens—rich or poor

_____ a cure for cancer

_____ medical care for persons with AIDS

_____ massive government-sponsored television spots to educate the public on the dangers of smoking, drugs, fatty diets, and the lack of exercise

_____ increased Medicare payments for the elderly

_____ increasing health care for people in poor nations

_____ developing even more sophisticated medical technology

_____ educating teens about the dangers of premarital pregnancy

_____ teaching the public about the value of a simple lifestyle and its contribution to health

Part 2: **Research Project**. Find at least three references on one of the following topics. Make sure one of your references presents church teaching. Then prepare a short oral presentation that includes 1) a definition of the topic; 2) some of the ethical issues involved; 3) current church teaching; and 4) your own opinion.

Topics:

euthanasia
abortion
genetic engineering
cloning
cryogenics
in vitro fertilization

organ transplants
surrogate motherhood
artificial insemination (husband)
the "living will"
research involving human subjects
newborns with birth defects

38. Capital Punishment: Right or Wrong?

Traditional Church Teaching:

1. All human life is sacred—God's gift to give and to take away. *But,*

2. Innocent persons who are unjustly attacked have the right to defend themselves against unjust aggressors. They must use the minimum amount of force necessary to stop the assailant and must never be revengeful.

3. By extension, society has the right to defend itself by means of capital punishment against those who have committed serious crimes. In other words, as St. Thomas Aquinas writes, "If a person is dangerous and destructive to the community on account of some sin, it is praiseworthy and healthy that he be killed in order that the common good be preserved."

For Capital Punishment

1. All actions have consequences; rapists, murderers, kidnappers, and the like should realize that there is a price to pay for serious crimes.

2. Severe punishment, like the death penalty, will *deter* others from committing the same kind of crime. Potential criminals will think twice before killing, raping, kidnapping.

3. When a wrong is committed, justice must balance the scales. An eye-for-an-eye, a tooth-for-a-tooth. Society needs to protect itself.

4. It is better for a prisoner to die than to rot in a prison for a lifetime.

Against Capital Punishment

1. Show mercy to the sinner. People can always repent and change. You can't reform a dead person.

2. There is not indisputable proof that capital punishment actually deters crime. In fact, the first public lynching in England for pickpocketing, the thieves went wild picking the pockets of the spectators.

3. Capital punishment discriminates against the poor who cannot hire the best lawyers to argue their case.

4. The goal of our correctional system is to rehabilitate the criminal, not kill him or her.

CHOOSING

■ *discuss* ■

1. Are these valid arguments?
2. Divide into "pro" and "con" groups. Research some of the above, then have small-group discussions on these issues.
3. Is capital punishment or life imprisonment economically cheaper?

Capital Punishment: The Church's Emerging Position

In working toward a consistent pro-life ethic, many church leaders say that in our day it is not possible to justify capital punishment. They have studied the church's traditional teaching and have concluded that society has changed. Circumstances are such that there are suitable alternatives to capital punishment, ones that show our commitment to God's gift of life.

Christians of good will might disagree with this emerging teaching, but they must seriously study and pray over the points the bishops make in coming to their new conclusion about capital punishment.

1. Although society has the *right* and *duty* to defend itself, capital punishment is not the *only* way to accomplish this end. Human life is sacred. A civilized society has other ways to defend itself short of the death penalty.

2. Research indicates that many potential criminals are not deterred by threat of the death penalty.

3. The death penalty is disproportionally administered to poor persons and members of minority groups. (The rich also commit violent crimes, but they have the means to wrest as much advantage as they can out of the criminal justice system.)

4. Sometimes mistakes are made and innocent people are executed. These mistakes can never be corrected.

5. The Christian must stand for the protection of *all* life. To forgive the criminal and work toward his or her rehabilitation is a great sign of love. Too often capital punishment has been administered out of motives of revenge. Revenge can never be the motive for a Christian, who must forgive.

6. To be against capital punishment is not to be against punishment of the criminal. A dangerous, anti-social person must be removed from society for the common good. Incarceration gives the criminal the opportunity to repent and reform.

7. Compassion must be shown to the victims of crime.

8. Christians must focus on the societal conditions that cause crime and reform the penal system, which is often a breeding place for even more crime.

▪ *discuss* ▪

1. What three crimes would you judge deserving of the most serious punishment?

2. Recommend some types of punishment in place of capital punishment.

CHOOSING

39. Capital Punishment: The Night Stalker

One of the most horrendous cases of serial killing was that of the so-called Night Stalker, sentenced by a California jury to die in the gas chamber for his thirteen satanic murders.

His defending attorney argued for life imprisonment, saying that would be punishment enough for him. "Life imprisonment without possibility of parole means he will never see Disneyland again," said the lawyer. "He will never be free again."

However, the jury voted for death on each of the special circumstances attached to the accused's murder convictions. The Night Stalker was also convicted of thirty felonies including burglaries and sex crimes. During testimony, the following was revealed:

- The murderer mercilessly slashed his victims' throats.
- He gouged out the eyes of one woman.
- He killed for self-gratification.
- He left satanic symbols at the scene of some of his slayings.
- He forced some of his victims to swear by Satan and beg for mercy.
- During his trial he held up his hand inscribed with a satanic symbol and said, "Hail Satan."
- When the verdict was delivered, he said, "See you in Disneyland." Then, he flashed a satanic sign and said "Evil."

■ discuss ■

1. The defense attorney in this case said, "I think all human beings are deserving of our sympathy and should not have their lives taken in the streets, in the courts, or in the gas chamber." Do you agree?
2. Is there such a thing as a thoroughly evil person? Explain.
3. Was this man sick? If so, should he be executed?
4. Other than capital punishment, what would be a fitting punishment for this criminal?
5. What would Jesus say about this case? Suppose he were a jury member. How might he argue?

40. The Crying Baby

One of the most popular TV programs ever was M*A*S*H. Its last episode drew an enormous viewing audience. It contained the following moral dilemma:

> Hawkeye—one of the doctor-heroes of the show—was on a bus with some fellow surgeons and a few Koreans. He informed the driver of the bus that some enemy soldiers were approaching, and the bus should be hidden on the side of the road.
> As the enemy soldiers were walking by the bus, an infant in the bus began to cry.

What was the mother to do in this situation? What should she do? Should she muffle the baby (risking suffocating her child) to keep the occupants of the bus from being discovered? Or should she allow the baby to breathe (and cry) and thus risk discovery and possible death for all the people on the bus?

■ discuss ■

1. What should the mother do?
2. What would *you* do?
3. What would Jesus require in this situation?
4. Are many lives worth more than one life? Is it ever moral to sacrifice one life for the many?

41. Euthanasia: Church Teaching

Euthanasia, literally "happy or good death" means "an act or method of causing death painlessly, so as to end suffering." There are two basic types:

a. *Active (positive or direct) euthanasia*: The directly willed inducement of death for merciful reasons. (This is the term most people mean when they use the word *euthanasia*.) **This is forbidden by the church.**

b. *Passive (negative or indirect) euthanasia*: Allowing oneself or another to die; for example, when the person is terminally ill, where there is no obligation to continue life-support systems, and where there is no reasonable hope for recovery. This is confusing because most people mean active euthanasia, not this passive euthanasia, when they are debating this issue.

Church teaching:

1. *Life is sacred.* Each person has basic dignity because he or she is a child of God made in God's image. No one has an absolute right over his or her life. We belong to God and to each other.

2. *We must take all **ordinary** means to preserve life.* Individuals and society must do all that is reasonably necessary to preserve and safeguard God's gift of human life. However, we are not obligated to use *extraordinary* means to prolong life when there appears to be no hope for the individual. (However, we may use extraordinary means if we wish to do so.) Gerald Ford, S J, describes ordinary means and extraordinary means this way:

a. *ordinary means*: "not only normal food, drink, and rest but all medicines, treatments, and operations which offer a reasonable hope of benefit and which can be obtained and used without excessive pain or other inconvenience";

b. *extraordinary means*: "all medicines, treatments, and operations, which cannot be obtained without excessive expense, pain, or other inconvenience, or which, if used, would not offer a reasonable hope of benefit."[1]

Ordinary means would also include any means necessary to ease pain and discomfort, and to assist the patient in being lucid and alert.

Extraordinary means would be very costly, very unusual, very painful, very difficult, very dangerous, or would achieve very little good in the long run.

3. *We may not directly kill a person.* In other words, *active euthanasia is immoral.* "Whatever is opposed to life itself, such as any type of murder, genocide, abortion, euthanasia, or willful self-destruction, whatever violates the integrity of the human person, such as mutilation, torments inflicted on body or mind, attempts to coerce the will itself; whatever insults human dignity,

such as subhuman living conditions, arbitrary imprisonment, deportation, slavery, prostitution, the selling of women and children; as well as disgraceful working conditions, where [people] are treated as mere tools for profit rather than as free and responsible persons; all these things and others of their like are infamies indeed. They poison human society, but they do more harm to those who practice them than those who suffer from the injury. Moreover, they are a supreme dishonor to the Creator" (*Pastoral Constitution on the Church in the Modern World*, No. 27).

4. *A person has the right to meet a natural death in peace.* We are not obligated to use extraordinary means to maintain life at any cost. Christian faith holds that death is not the end of human existence; rather, it is a transition to a new, glorious life with the risen Lord. Christians also believe that the evil of suffering can be transformed into something good when it is joined to the redemptive suffering of the Lord Jesus.

Application Questions:

1. Suppose a woman discovers a lump in her breast. Is she obligated to have it examined?

2. Does a man dying of acute leukemia have to participate in experimental treatments to prolong his life?

3. Discuss whether heart transplants should be considered ordinary or extraordinary means.

4. Would administering a drug to stop a suffering person's breathing be considered active or passive euthanasia?

5. Let's say a patient were comatose for two years, supported by a respirator. Would it be active euthanasia to take the person off the machine?

6. Read over the quotation from Vatican II given above. Would it be moral to use torture to extract information from a proven traitor?

---

[1] Gerald Ford, S.J., in John Dedek, *Human Life: Some Moral Issues* (Mission, KS: Sheed Andrews and McMeel, 1972), pp.125-26.

42. Gramps

Your grandfather, age eighty-two, has been living with your family for the past five years, ever since your grandmother died and left him alone. He has a severe case of arthritis and is usually in severe pain. He has now developed liver cancer, a painful, terminal condition. He has been in the hospital recently, but has come home to the family as he awaits death.

At most, the doctors give him four months to live.

One evening your parents are out for the evening. It is your turn to look after your grandfather. He calls you into his room and begins to talk to you. He tells you that he knows he is at the end of his life, and he is ready to go. But he confesses that he can't stand the pain of his disease. In listening to him you are convinced that he is in such a frame of mind that he would take his life if given the chance. After calming him down and reassuring him of your love, you leave his room.

Around an hour later, Gramps yells out in pain. You rush into his room. He begs you to give him his bottle of sleeping pills and a glass of water. The family has always kept his medicine locked up in the medicine cabinet fearing that Grandpa might one day try to take his life.

You look at the pain in your grandfather's eyes and hear it in his voice. You are convinced that if you give him his bottle of sleeping pills he will take them all. What would you do?

■ *discuss* ■

1. What alternatives are open to you in this case? What are the consequences of each one?

2. If you gave your grandfather what he requested and he did overdose on the pills, would you share some guilt for his death? Would you be guilty of murder?

3. When a pet is gravely ill or badly wounded, it is often killed to put it out of its pain. Why does Catholic morality say that the same standards can't be applied to human life?

4. Assume a person's brain has ceased functioning (a clinical sign that death has taken place.) Discuss the morality of keeping a person's body on a respirator and other equipment in order to use it as a source for body parts.

5. Suppose a man develops a brain tumor. The doctors tell him that if it is not operated on, he will die in six months. But they also tell him if they do operate, there is a 90 percent chance he will be deaf and blind. Must the man undergo the operation?

43. Bomb Shelter

Directions:
1. Divide into small groups. Pretend your country is being attacked by a foreign nation. Each group is in charge of the shelter in its district. Ten people want to get in, but there is room for only six.
2. First, make your own personal choices. Then decide in your small group who will be admitted to the shelter.

The ten people are:

a. your mother

b. a female doctor who has performed 500 abortions, age forty-five

c. a famous botanist who is infected with the AIDS virus but has shown no symptoms yet, male, age thirty-five

d. a slightly retarded teen-age girl, age sixteen

e. a wealthy and famous rock guitarist, male, age twenty-four

f. a nun who has worked twenty years with battered women, age fifty-four

g. a healthy, strong marine, age nineteen

h. an author who has written many psychological self-help books, male, age sixty-two

i. a carpenter, male, age thirty

j. your best friend

■ *discuss* ■

- What criteria did your group use to make its choices? Were these rational (based on reason) or emotional?

- What prejudices surfaced in the discussion? How did your group deal with them? Did they affect the choices?

- Many people observe that our government assumes the same role you played in this game. Because of its economic decisions, some people simply cannot survive in our society. Do you agree or disagree? Offer evidence.

44. Guns

The mayor of a medium-sized city is running for re-election taking the position that an armed populace is a strong deterrent to crime. He says, "Every home should have a weapon to protect its inhabitants." He claims that arming is a constitutional right and has urged his city commission to adopt a resolution to declare war on crime.

The police chief, appointed by the mayor, is against the idea. The chief says that "when a community arms itself, you are asking for trouble."

■ *questions* ■

1. Who is right on this issue? Where do you personally stand on the possession of weapons?

2. List and discuss three arguments for and against the mayor's position:

For	*Against*
a. _____	a. _____
b. _____	b. _____
c. _____	c. _____

3. Based on a Christian understanding of the real identity of humans, would the mayor's position be right or wrong? Explain.

CHOOSING

45. Moral Dilemmas: Life and Death Issues

Directions: Consider the following principles in deciding the dilemmas given below.

- All life is a gift from God and should be respected. The fifth commandment forbids any direct attack on another human person's life.
- Catholic morality permits us to use force to defend ourselves against unjust aggressors.
- We must use reasonable means to preserve our life and the lives of others.
- We are all brothers and sisters. No one has to earn the right to life. It is a God-given right.

Suppose you found out that a pharmacist filled a prescription with the wrong drug. A ninety-year-old woman died as a result. The pharmacist has never made a mistake like this before. He is an upright, moral person with a fine reputation. Would you inform the authorities? Should you inform the authorities?

Your beautiful, intelligent, and highly ethical girlfriend was kidnapped, raped, mutilated, and murdered. A serial rapist is finally caught and convicted. He is condemned to die in the electric chair. An anti-capital punishment group asks you to march with it to protest the execution. Could you? Should you?

A baby born with Down's syndrome also has a blockage between the stomach and the intestines. If not operated on soon, the baby will die. The operation is rather easy and safe to do. Must the parents order the operation? Must the doctor perform the operation regardless of the wishes of the parents? Explain.

Triage is a method for deciding whom to treat when there are insufficient medical supplies and personnel for treatment of all the injured. For example, medical personnel treat soldiers according to their chances of survival. Others may be left untreated to die or make it as best they can.

Suppose you were the doctor in charge of making medical decisions at a hospital near the front lines. It is up to you to make triage decisions.

While engaged in this work, your near-dead brother is brought in. His chances of survival are about 10 percent, but expert, immediate care *might* save his life. If you treat him, other, less injured soldiers, will be left untreated. Some of them will probably die.

Would you violate military policies and treat your brother? Explain.

■ *discussion* ■

1. Does society value some individual lives over others? Explain with examples.

2. In the triage case, discuss some possible alternatives besides those implied in the case.

3. Can revenge ever be a motive for Christians in defending their lives? Explain.

4. Should the perpetrator of every wrongful death be punished in some way to give an example to others that life must be respected regardless of the circumstances? (Discuss this in light of the pharmacist case.)

46. Peace or War?

If asked, most people would say they want peace in their country and in the world. But not everyone agrees on how to bring about or guarantee that peace. Where do you stand on the questions of war and peace? Check your view in the proper column. Then share and defend your choices.

	Agree	Dis-agree	No Opinion
1. Strong, free countries are obligated to come to the defense of unjustly attacked weaker nations.			
2. A pacifist is unpatriotic.			
3. Military strength is the best insurance for peace.			
4. The United States has never fought an unjust war.			
5. All wars are evil.			
6. War heroes are more popular than peace heroes.			
7. Periodic wars are necessary for population control and to deal with humanity's aggressive instinct.			
8. There always have been wars and there always will be wars.			

	Agree	Dis-agree	No Opinion
9. If a nation must have a military draft, then women as well as men should be subject to it.			
10. Young people can be trained for peace as well as they are trained for war.			

■ *discuss* ■

1. In one of the Beatitudes, Jesus blesses peacemakers. Can you be a follower of Jesus and still participate in a war? Explain.
2. "Peace begins with me." As a group, describe five common conflict situations young people often encounter. Then suggest several ways each of these conflicts can be resolved *peacefully*.
3. Under what conditions would you kill another person?

Research: Obtain a copy of the American bishops' peace pastoral, *The Challenge of Peace.* Read the opening section of the letter, which includes a summary, some principles and norms, and additional moral principles dealing with policy choices. Then go through each of the statements above and decide how the bishops would mark them.

47. Respect Life!

There are many ways of showing respect for life. There are people who would say that each of the following statements must be upheld if a person really respects life. Maybe that is true—and maybe not. Mark 1 if you agree with the following, 2 if you disagree or 3 if you don't know what your position is.

_____ 1. The arms race is an unspeakable crime against humanity; all steps must be taken to stop it.

_____ 2. There should be stricter laws to ban the possession of all firearms.

_____ 3. Regardless of the circumstance, no one should ever kill another human being.

_____ 4. Killing animals for sport is clearly wrong. (Killing animals for food or clothing is another issue.)

_____ 5. The most serious moral crime of the last twenty years is abortion.

_____ 6. Recreational drug use is wrong because it endangers the mental, physical, and emotional health of a creature of God.

_____ 7. Doctors should use all ordinary and reasonable means to keep people alive, regardless of their age or mental condition.

_____ 8. Capital punishment is wrong because it is revengeful and plays at being God.

_____ 9. Boxing should be outlawed as a sport because its only object is to hurt the opponent.

_____ 10. Since life is God's gift, people should not smoke cigarettes.

■ Share your responses with other members of your group. Justify your choices. Did anyone choose 1 for all the items?

■ Discuss each item to see what the statement is trying to get at. Then rewrite it in such a way that 75 percent of your group can agree with it.

Research: Jesus respected life. The following texts show how Jesus acted toward others or present his teaching on how we should act toward others. In small groups of four or so, look up these texts and then draft a statement about how we should relate to others.

Matthew:	5:38-48	7:1-5	25:31-40
Luke:	15:11-32	23:32	23:39-43
John:	1:40-42	5:1-15	9:36-37

48. Suicide

Suicide, the deliberate taking of one's own life, is a serious problem. It is a major cause of death among teenagers, following only accidents. Undoubtedly, many people who commit this tragic act do so because they are emotionally disturbed or their perception of reality is distorted. These conditions limit their freedom to choose.

Restriction of freedom does, of course, lessen one's moral blameworthiness. However, even in the case of suicide, it is possible for people to commit it with freedom and knowledge of what they are doing. Some people reason that suicide enables them to control their own lives, and they use it as an escape from a life they judge as not worthy of living.

Christianity has rejected suicide as a gross disrespect for God's precious gift of life. St. Thomas Aquinas argued that suicide is a crime against society, depriving it of one of its members. As social beings, the victims of suicide have cut themselves from the community of humans who have brought them into existence and sustained them. Suicide also hurts family and loved ones and discourages them in their own task of living.

Christians reject suicide because we cherish God's great gift of life. It is not a commodity that we can dispose of as we see fit.

But what is suicide? Read the following cases and discuss them.

Case #1: A friend of yours has been giving away some of her favorite possessions. She seems depressed lately. Things are tough at home, school, and work. Her boyfriend of six months has just dropped her. She talks as though no one would miss her if she died. Last night she mentioned a few things that make you think that she might do something drastic, but she made you promise not to tell anyone what she has confided to you. You suspect she is suicidal.

What would you say to her? What would you do?

Case #2: Maximilian Kolbe volunteered to take the place of a family man who had been condemned to a starvation bunker by the Nazis. His offer was accepted, and Father Kolbe died in the bunker two weeks later. The man he saved lived to witness the canonization of *Saint* Maximilian Kolbe.

What is the difference between martyrdom and suicide?

Case #3: A twenty-four-year-old man poured gasoline over himself and lit a match in front of the United Nations Building. He did it to protest the lack of social justice for the poor nations of the world. His death was swift, but excruciatingly painful.

What principle of Catholic morality might have been violated here?

49. Teen suicide[2]

Facts

- 5,000 teens kill themselves every year.
- 500,000 teens *attempt* to kill themselves.
- You probably know someone who feels desperate enough to take his or her own life.
- The victims of suicide include family members, friends, and all others touched by the person's death; their loss cannot be measured.

Myths

- *People who try suicide are crazy.* No, most of them feel powerless and hopeless. They don't know where to turn.
- *People who talk about suicide, never do it.* Wrong. Anyone who talks about it is looking for help.
- *People who consider suicide will never be okay.* Not true. With professional help, teens can replace feelings of hopelessness with a positive self-image.

Warning Signs

1. A previous suicide attempt.
2. Talk or thoughts of suicide or death.
3. Changes in personality or mood.
4. Changes in eating or sleeping patterns.
5. Withdrawal from friends and activities.
6. Taking unusual risks.
7. Drug abuse.
8. Final arrangements—giving away prized possessions and making peace with friends.

How to Help

- Don't be quiet about this even if a friend has sworn you to secrecy. His or her life is at stake!
- Involve an adult immediately.
- If you think your friend is in danger, don't leave him or her alone!
- If you need time to get help, make a "contract" with your friend not to do anything until he or she has met with you again.

> **Check the phone book and write your local suicide prevention number here:**

Linda[3]

Linda failed to return home from a dance Friday night. On Saturday she told her family she had spent the night with an Air Force lieutenant.

Her parents decided on a punishment that would "wake Linda up." They ordered her to shoot the dog she had owned for about two years.

On Sunday, the parents and Linda drove the dog into the desert near their home. They had the girl dig a shallow grave. Then her mother grasped the dog's head between her hands and her father gave his daughter a .22 caliber pistol and told her to shoot the dog.

Instead, the girl put the pistol to her right temple and shot herself. The police said there were no charges that could be filed against the parents except possibly cruelty to animals.

Based on solid principles of Christian morality, judge what immoral actions (if any) were committed by each of the following:

- Linda
- the lieutenant
- her parents
- the police

> ■ *discuss* ■
>
> Which of the actions in this tragic case most seriously disrupts the love relationship with God and others?

---

[2] Some of the information on this page is taken from Janet Kolehmainen and Sandra Handwerk, *Teen Suicide* (Minneapolis: Lerner, 1986). This is a clear and short book for you to read.

[3] Jeffrey Schrank quotes this story in *Teaching Human Beings: 101 Subversive Activities for the Classroom* (Boston: Beacon Press, 1972), pp. 66-68. He excerpted it from Julius Lester, *Search for a New Land* (New York: Dial Press, 1968).

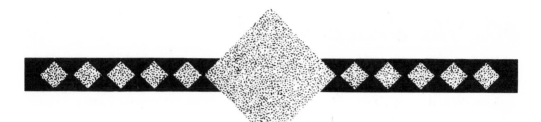

section six

Justice Issues

The Bible instructs us to do justice and love mercy. Democratic nations are built on the concept of equal justice for all. Pope Paul VI once wrote that you cannot have peace without justice.

Justice implies moral rightness, fair play, honor. Justice gives to each person what is his or her due by right. Justice is necessary for people to live in society in a harmonious, civil way.

Yet, rarely do we see justice served as God desires. We must constantly strive to act justly if we want to preserve the dignity of other persons.

50. The Environment

The automobile industry is vitally important to the economy of Western nations. Yet, it is threatened by nations which draw on cheaper labor. These nations are able to produce a quality car due to excellent work habits and pride in craftsmanship.

Contributing to the sluggishness of the domestic industry is the ever-stricter air pollution control standards and safety measures required by the federal government. Economists have admitted that the additional costs for physically safer and more ecologically sound cars have contributed to a slow-down in the auto manufacturing industry.

The result of stiff competition and strict standards has been factory shut-downs and job layoffs. Throughout the Mid-Western United States, for example, this phenomenon is so common that the region is called the "rust belt."

What can be done about the unemployment and human suffering caused by all of this? Some people suggest that the government slacken its standards for emission control and safety standards so cars could be made more cheaply and sold more competitively. People would be put back to work, there would be less unemployment, and the interest rates would probably decline.

The question: Should safety and environmental standards be lowered in order to help a domestic industry?

■ discuss ■

1. Where should governments draw the line to protect the environment and the lives of its citizens?

2. Should governments stay away from practices that might hurt employment?

3. What kind of responsibility do governments have to future generations? Should they restrict gasoline consumption (for example, through a heavy-use tax) in order to preserve supplies for the next generation? Should they greatly restrict the burning of fossil fuels?

4. Is it morally wrong to dismantle pollution-control devices on a car to get better gas mileage? Explain.

5. Is it *morally* wrong not to use a seat belt in a car?

51. Justice

Justice: rendering to each person what is his or her due by right

Here are two lists on justice topics. Rank each list from (1) the most severe violation of justice to (5) the least severe or no violation to justice.

List A

_____ A disgruntled student steals the English teacher's grade book near the end of the term. The teacher has no other source to establish student grades.

_____ A school system glorifies sports, but mostly those of male participants. Eighty percent of the athletic budget goes to male sports and 75 percent of that to only two sports: football and basketball.

_____ A student is denied access to the local Catholic high school because his parents are active in the pro-abortion movement.

_____ A teen is involved in a slight accident with a parked car late at night on a dark street. It is a dangerous neighborhood. She leaves the scene of the accident without leaving any word of who was responsible.

_____ A student is praised for his brilliant comment in class. He got the idea from a friend in another class, but does not mention that the idea was not original.

List B

_____ Professional athletes command huge salaries while teachers and safety personnel are chronically underpaid.

_____ Continual use of air conditioners in automobiles causes a threat to the ozone layer.

_____ The burdens of poverty in the United States of America fall most heavily on Blacks, Hispanics, and Native Americans. Moreover, children are the largest single group among the poor.

_____ Half the world's people live in countries where the per capita income is $400 or less.

_____ In China married couples may have no more than one child. Violation of this law requires forced sterilization.

1. The first set of cases deals with issues in personal justice. These topics deal with *fairness*. How would you define this term? What are some results for societies where fairness is not protected?

2. The second set of cases deals with social-justice topics. What is the most severe social injustice of our day in the following areas:

   a. Your city
   b. Your nation
   c. The world

3. As a group, list some inherent, inalienable rights each person has by the mere fact that he or she is a child of God, made in God's image. Here are some categories:

   a. social rights   c. political rights
   b. economic rights   d. religious rights

4. The American bishops' pastoral letter *Economic Justice for All* teaches that all economic issues should be judged from the perspective of their impact on the poor. What does this mean?

Research:

1. Obtain a copy of *Economic Justice for All*.

2. Read one of the following sections in this pastoral letter:

   a. Employment (paragraphs #136-69)
   b. Poverty (#170-215)
   c. Food and Agriculture (#216-59)

3. Create an outline based on the following points:

   a. Three important facts about the scope of the problem
   b. Three guidelines for responsible action
   c. Your opinion about the approaches the bishops recommend

52. More on Justice

> *Directions*:   Check the box that indicates your opinion on the following items. Your choices are agree (**A**), disagree (**D**) or no opinion (**?**).

	A	D	?
1. Any private club, for example, an athletic club, must be open to members of both sexes.			
2. As a member of a neighborhood association, you should have the right to refuse to allow certain "undesirables" to buy a home in your neighborhood.			
3. The government should provide financial support to women who want abortions in the cases of rape and incest.			
4. A quota system to benefit women and members of minorities is a way for some professional schools, such as medical school, to redress past injustices to members of these minorities.			
5. If a person has the academic ability, he or she then has the right to a college education, a right that the government must guarantee with financial aid.			
6. It is acceptable for police forces to fire overweight officers to insure their safety and that of the populace.			
7. To deter the selling of drugs in schools, school officials have the right to open and search students' lockers without their permission.			
8. Every person has the right to basic health insurance regardless of their ability to pay.			
9. It is morally wrong for Americans to waste food while half the world's population goes to bed hungry each night.			

■ *discussion* ■

1. What is the difference between a privilege and a right? Which of the above cases involve privileges?

2. What duties do citizens owe their governments? their employers?

3. What responsibilities should governments owe their citizens? What do employers owe their employees?

4. What individual rights can never be sacrificed for the common good?

53. Moral Dilemmas: Issues in Personal Integrity

Directions: Dilemmas involve situations that seem to defy satisfactory solutions. There seem to be pro and con reasons for acting one way or another.

Here are some situations that deal with personal honesty and integrity. Put yourself in the situation and determine what and how you would decide. You might consider the following principles of Christian morality:

- A good end does not justify evil means to attain it.

- Does what I propose to do make me more loving?

- Are there any other alternatives to the options suggested in the dilemma?

- What if everyone in a similar situation did what I propose to do? Would the consequences be good or bad?

- I am a child of God, made in God's image. Am I reflecting God in this action?

Bribe: Would you pay bribes to foreign officials to gain sales for your company?

Fraternity: You are a freshman in college. As an initiation rite to join a fraternity, you are expected to shoplift an item worth at least $5 from a grocery store. Would you?

Help Yourself: It is a common practice for travelers to take things like ashtrays and towels from motel rooms. These items are small and not worth a tremendous amount of money. In fact, some people argue that their cost is built into the room rental rate. Motels and hotels *expect* them to be taken. Do you think it is stealing to take items like these? Why or why not?

The Letter: You find a letter in the hallway at school. It is marked confidential. You decide to open it. It is from the principal to the department chairman of history informing the chairman that the school is not going to renew your favorite history teacher's contract for next school year. The principal asks the chairman to keep this news confidential until the school year ends because he doesn't want to have to deal with students who will most certainly come to the defense of the teacher. What would you do?

Wallet: Suppose you found the wallet of a classmate. It contains $35. This particular classmate has owed you $20 for the past six months and has ignored all your pleas to repay the loan. What would you do?

Tip: Suppose you are a waitress in a rather up-scale restaurant. The wealthy patron meant to leave you a $20 tip, but instead left a $100 bill. Would you notify the person of his mistake? Should you?

■ discussion ■

Discuss your responses with members of your group.

1. What kind of effort must you make to return lost property?
2. Is it wrong to engage in business practices (for example, exaggerating claims about a product) that seem common practice and are understood by everyone to be less than honest?
3. What does it mean to steal?
4. Discuss several situations where you would *never* be dishonest.

54. Prejudice

Prejudice, judging based on insufficient data, is one of the great moral issues of every age. The harm it causes others is beyond measure.

Prejudice often manifests itself in stereotypical thinking. A stereotype is an oversimplification that results in a generalization. Stereotyping can be favorable, but rarely is; it is usually uncomplimentary or even degrading.

Here are some statements. Check off those that appear to be stereotypes, conclusions based on prejudiced thinking.

_____ 1. Some welfare recipients are dishonest. Thus, the government should periodically review its procedures for applying for welfare.

_____ 2. Women are not cut out for careers in the construction industry, police and fire protection, and work in steel mills. These are men's jobs.

_____ 3. Drug addicts come from low-class backgrounds.

_____ 4. Homosexuals should be banned from the classroom because they are known to seduce children.

_____ 5. Students of Oriental backgrounds have achieved higher math scores in recent years on certain standardized tests.

_____ 6. Women who are the victims of rape usually deserve it. It's the way they dress and act that shows they are asking for it.

_____ 7. Our judicial system works better if you are white, male, and wealthy.

_____ 8. People who are poor pretty much deserve their lot in life. If they'd work hard they could escape their poverty.

Research:

Statements 1, 5, and 7 above are probably not stereotypes. Using a reliable resource, choose one of these statements and find some facts to substantiate it. Or choose one of the stereotypes and find some reliable information to disprove it. Share the results of your research with your group.

■ *discuss* ■

1. What stereotypes have you or any of your friends been victimized by? How do you think these generalizations got started?

2. What stereotypes does society have about the following groups:

- professional athletes
- rock musicians
- parents
- teachers
- doctors
- Blacks
- lawyers

- overweight people
- alcoholics
- persons with AIDS
- old people
- Hispanics
- teens
- Catholics

Discuss responses you can make to any of the stereotypes you came up with.

Directions: Here are the beginnings of some common stereotypes. Complete them based on your own judgments or those you think are common among your classmates.

1. _____ are lazy.

2. _____ are only interested in making money.

3. _____ get the best grades because they are so grade-conscious.

4. _____ are the best athletes.

5. _____ all look alike.

6. _____ are _____.

Questions:

- Do you think most stereotypes are based on reason or emotion? Give examples.

- What are the effects of stereotyping? How can it be overcome?

- From a Christian point of view, give several reasons why prejudice is wrong.

55. Rights

A right is a claim we can make on others and society in order to live a fully human life. A right does not have to be earned; it is something due us because we are God's children made in God's image and likeness. Here is a list of so-called rights. Judge whether you agree that they are indeed rights.

	Yes	No	?
1. Do gay people have the right to adopt children?	☐	☐	☐
2. Does a seventeen-year-old have the right to drink alcoholic beverages?	☐	☐	☐
3. Do police officers and fire fighters have the right to strike?	☐	☐	☐
4. Do convicted criminals have the right to watch television in prison?	☐	☐	☐
5. Do mothers have the right to tax benefits in order to stay at home and raise children?	☐	☐	☐
6. Does a terminally ill, comatose person have the right to be disconnected from life-support systems?	☐	☐	☐
7. Does a poor person have the right to a Catholic high-school education?	☐	☐	☐
8. Does an underdeveloped, exploited nation have the right to nuclear weapons for self-defense?	☐	☐	☐
9. Do women have the right to jobs in the construction industry?	☐	☐	☐
10. Does a person have the right to belong to a cult that worships Satan?	☐	☐	☐

■ *discuss* ■

1. Defend your choices. Then, as a group, construct a list of "inalienable rights" that you all agree on.
2. "Every right has a corresponding duty." For every right you list, state a duty that goes along with that particular right.

56. More on Rights

In his famous encyclical, *Pacem in Terris* (*Peace on Earth*), Pope John XXIII teaches the basis of all human rights and duties:

Any human being, if it is to be well-ordered and productive, must lay down as a foundation this principle: that every human being is a person; his nature is endowed with intelligence and free will. By virtue of this, he has rights and duties of his own, flowing directly and simultaneously from his very nature, which are therefore universal, inviolable and inalienable.

If we look upon the dignity of the human person in the light of divinely revealed truth, we cannot help but esteem it far more highly; for men are redeemed by the blood of Jesus Christ, they are by grace the children and friends of God and heirs of eternal glory (*Pacem in Terris*, Nos. 9-10).

This important quote reminds us that rights are due us as God's children. Governments and institutions have a corresponding duty to guarantee basic human rights and see that they are fulfilled through private or governmental action. Individuals also have a corresponding duty to exercise their rights responsibly.

Here is a list of various rights. Identify them according to the following: E=economic; P=political; C=cultural. In the space to the right, briefly mention a corresponding duty for that particular right.

_____ 1. the right to a decent education   _____

_____ 2. the right to vote   _____

_____ 3. the right to equal access to a given job   _____

_____ 4. the right to a living wage   _____

_____ 5. the right to a speedy trial   _____

_____ 6. the right to worship God as one sees fit   _____

_____ 7. the right to marry and plan the size of one's family   _____

_____ 8. the right to assembly   _____

_____ 9. the right to develop one's God-given talents   _____

_____ 10. the right to security in case of sickness   _____

_____ 11. the right to food, shelter, and clothing   _____

_____ 12. the right to life   _____

_____ 13. the right to choose one's friends   _____

_____ 14. the right to private property   _____

■ *discussion* ■

As a group, come up with a list of ten rights every teenager should have. Identify each of these as political, economic, or social. Then list a corresponding duty for each of these rights.

57. Research Project: World Hunger

The right to have a share of earthly goods sufficient for oneself and one's family belongs to everyone. The Fathers and Doctors of the Church held this view, teaching that all are obliged to come to the relief of the poor, and to do so not merely out of their superfluous goods. If a person is in extreme necessity, he has the right to take from the riches of others what he himself needs. Since there are so many people in the world afflicted by hunger, this Sacred Council urges all, both individuals and governments, to remember the saying of the Fathers: Feed the man dying of hunger, because if you have not fed him you have killed him (*Constitution on the Church in the Modern World, No. 69*).

Part 1: Research

A. Select one of the following countries to represent.

Afghanistan	Czechoslovakia	Norway
Algeria	Dominican Republic	Pakistan
Argentina	Ethiopia	Poland
Austria	France	Spain
Belize	Guatemala	Sri Lanka
Brazil	Haiti	Thailand
Burma	Iraq	U.S.S.R.
Cambodia	Ireland	U.S.A.
Canada	Japan	Great Britain
China	Mexico	Zimbabwe

B. Using a world almanac, current encyclopedias, yearbooks, and the like, research the following:

1. Current population
2. Geography and topography of the country
3. Economy: exports/imports
4. Per capita income
5. Life expectancy
6. Infant mortality
7. Literacy rate
8. Major religions of the country
9. Percent of the populace who go to bed hungry each night

Part 2: Share your information with your group. Then do the following:

1. Decide which five nations are the poorest and which five are the most well-off.
2. Brainstorm on ten ways the rich nations can help the poor nations.
3. Discuss some things the rich nations are currently doing to help the poorer nations. How can they do better?

58. Stewardship

Genesis reveals that God entrusted humans with the care of his beautiful creation. We must be good stewards who must prudently use, not foolishly abuse, the goods of this earth.

Please mark the following poll which deals with issues in stewardship. Discuss the questions that follow.

	Agree	Dis-agree	Don't Know
1. Western nations should fight the Oil Cartel by becoming energy sufficient, even if this means resorting to strip mining of coal.	☐	☐	☐
2. To increase crop output to help feed the poor of the world, nations should allow more liberal use of pesticides.	☐	☐	☐
3. The war on cancer and other deadly diseases is so crucial that medical personnel should be allowed to use experimental drugs on patients, even without their consent.	☐	☐	☐
4. Knowing that many technological advances happen because of space exploration, the government's top priority must be much greater spending on this important area.	☐	☐	☐
5. In harvesting natural resources, we can't be too concerned about endangered species. Human needs must come before the existence of certain animal and plant forms.	☐	☐	☐

■ discuss ■

1. List and discuss several negative effects of each of the above arguments. Discuss some examples of tampering with the laws of nature that you think are clearly wrong. (For example, what about testing nuclear weapons in the atmosphere?)

2. Are any of the statements above clearly immoral? If so, what moral principles might be violated? Explain.

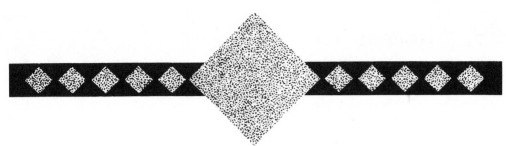

section seven

Christian Living

Jesus asks those who wish to follow him to pick up their crosses. Following in the footsteps of the Master is not easy. It demands discipline, steadfastness, and self-control. Sometimes we might even have to suffer to do what we know is right. But the payoff is great: friendship with Jesus and everlasting life with him in eternity.

How do you begin? Alcoholics Anonymous has a twelve-step plan for personal growth, renewal, and control. These steps have a profoundly religious foundation. Many people have found in them a blueprint for virtuous living. To bring out their spiritual base, here are several of them in a rewritten form:

- You are powerless without God. Only God can give you strength to live a good life. Surrender yourself to God.

- Examine your heart. Admit to God that you are a sinner. Promise to begin to amend your life. Ask God to help you.

- Make amends with all the people you have harmed.

- Continue to take stock of your spiritual and moral growth. Admit when you are wrong.

- Pray to God; stay in constant touch with God.

- Spread the good news of God's love to everyone you meet.

Turn now to some moral issues in Christian living.

59. Careers

People can grow holy through the work they do. In his encyclical *On Human Work (Laborem Exercens)*, Pope John Paul II writes:

> Work is a good thing for man—a good thing for his humanity—because through work man not only transforms nature, adapting it to his own needs, but he also achieves fulfillment as a human being and indeed in a sense becomes "more a human being" (No. 9).

Most of us admire hardworking people. At the same time, certain professions or jobs carry an aura of prestige while others are looked on as second-rate. Unfortunately, people sometimes don't think they are worthwhile because they don't have one of the jobs society considers praiseworthy.

What about you? How do you envision work, careers, your own future?

Here is a list of jobs/vocations. Rank them from the one you most admire (**1**) to the one you least admire (**18**).

____ teacher	____ secretary	____ priest
____ police officer	____ attorney	____ used-car salesperson
____ medical doctor	____ factory worker	____ bus driver
____ movie actress	____ nurse	____ waiter/waitress
____ full-time mother	____ politician	____ model
____ garbage collector	____ professional athlete	____ accountant

What job/vocation do you hope to be doing ten years from now?

Name three ways your choice can help you grow closer to God and others

a. _____   b. _____

c. _____

■ *discuss* ■

1. Do we tend to label people according to the work they do? If so, what are some dangers in labeling people this way?

2. For each of the professions/jobs listed above, come up with a list of three temptations to do immoral actions that might face a person in that particular vocation.

Christian Living

60. Letter #1

Everyone needs someone to talk to, to share his or her problems in life. Sometimes we write to a friend about our difficulties. Read the letter below, then respond to it.

Dear Alex,

I hate my parents and don't know what to do with them. They drive me crazy. Let me give you three examples.

First, I have a part-time job, which pays me around $60 a week. They take the check and deposit it in the bank and give me only $15 a week for allowance. They say the balance is for my college expenses. This is grossly unfair. All my friends get to keep whatever they earn for spending money.

Second, their curfew is absurd. They want me in at midnight every, and I repeat *every*, Friday and Saturday night. Not one of my friends has to be in before 1:00 a.m. There is no reasoning with them. If I don't get in on time, then I can't have the car for a whole month.

Third, they are religious freaks. I don't see anything wrong with skipping Mass one Sunday a month to get some shut-eye. But they literally drag me out of bed to go with them to Mass and Sunday brunch afterward. I'm really tired of the routine. Besides, Mass is getting to be pretty boring.

I think you can see my parents are pretty strict and awfully square. Any ideas on how to cope with them?

— **IMPRISONED IN IOWA**

Dear IMPRISONED:

■ *discuss* ■

1. Share and discuss what you wrote with your classmates.
2. Reach consensus on a list of five *reasonable* rules parents might expect sixteen- to eighteen-year-old teens to keep. Make another list of *unreasonable* rules. Discuss these. Show the lists to your parents and see if they agree with what you and your peers came up with.

61. Letter #2

Read and respond to the following letter.

Dear Alice,

I am almost ashamed of myself for having to write this letter to you. But today I finally decided to clean out my son's pigsty of a closet. I had told him that it was his responsibility to take care of his own room, but the mess finally got to me.

As I was rummaging through the disaster, a cigar box tipped over and three letters and what appeared to be a couple of joints fell out.

I read the letters. Two of them were harmless enough, letters from one of his friends who moved away last year. But the third was a real shocker. It was from my son's girlfriend, Kaye. She described in shocking detail the fun she had making love to my son a few weeks back. My heart sank into my feet. Anger, deep hurt, confusion, and helplessness raged inside me all at the same time.

What should I do? My first impulse is to confront him with the letter and the joints and bring the whole thing out in the open. But I'm afraid he won't ever trust me again—accusing me of snooping around.

Should I ignore all this and pray that the situation will correct itself? I'm not sure this is right either. I really need some advice.

— **SHOCKED AND HURT MOTHER**

Dear SHOCKED:

■ *discuss* ■

1. Do parents ever have a right to go through their teenager's personal possessions without their permission? If so, under what circumstances? What if the teenager had become withdrawn and uncommunicable after a close friend's suicide, for example? Would your answer be different?

2. Share responses to this letter. Ask your parents to give their views on this topic also.

62. Living Virtuously

Ben Franklin wrote in his *Autobiography* his plan for living a virtuous life. First, he listed and then defined thirteen virtues worth our effort to master. Next, he strove to master each virtue in turn, keeping track of his efforts in a little notebook. He discovered that he had many more faults than he imagined and that growth in the moral life is difficult. He also had an abundance of friends to help him see faults he never dreamed he had. But Franklin did notice some growth. He credited a nightly review of his day as a good way for him to measure any progress he made.

Why not try Franklin's plan for a week? Here are the four cardinal or moral virtues so important for growth in the Christian life. Put a check mark in the box opposite the virtue for each day you did something positive to enhance that virtue. In the column to the right, list one shortcoming for each day of the week and try to work on that the following day.

	Prudence	Justice	Temperance	Fortitude	
S	☐	☐	☐	☐	_____
M	☐	☐	☐	☐	_____
T	☐	☐	☐	☐	_____
W	☐	☐	☐	☐	_____
Th	☐	☐	☐	☐	_____
F	☐	☐	☐	☐	_____
S	☐	☐	☐	☐	_____

Prudence: moral common sense; the ability to discern proper moral behavior; (attitudes: being open minded; being prayerful; consulting others)

Justice: giving each person what is due him or her (attitudes: fair, honest; respecting others' rights; contributing to the welfare of others)

Temperance: moderation in food, drink, and sex (attitudes: using self-denial to build self-discipline; respecting own and others' sexuality; not abusing alcohol)

Fortitude: moral courage to deal with the difficulties in doing good (attitudes: doing something positive for others; resisting peer pressure)

Review: After reviewing the week, list your greatest strength and what you need most work on:

Strength: _____

Needs work: _____

63. Moral Compromise

A major obstacle to doing right is following the crowd, compromising our values for acceptance. How about you? On the following continuums, mark an **X** where you believe you are.

Would you...
1. Pick up litter in the school hallway when none of your friends do?

---
stand alone   **conform**

2. Go to daily Mass when none of your friends do?

---
stand alone   **conform**

3. Participate in a right-to-life rally against the wishes of your parents?

---
stand alone   **conform**

4. Turn in ten kids who are cheating on an exam? (Your class is on an honor system but no one else will turn them in.)

---
stand alone   **conform**

5. Stop to help an elderly bag lady who has fallen? No one else is stopping.

---
stand alone   **conform**

Politics and Money.   How would you solve this case? Discuss your response with members of your group.

It is the month of May and you badly need money to go to the spring dance with your special friend. As everyone knows, it is an expensive weekend. Right now you don't have a job or any outside source of income to raise the necessary funds for the dance and the fun weekend to follow.

However, a friend of yours tells you that you can earn $200 canvassing the local neighborhoods on three weekends in May working for a local politician. The politician is running in a tight primary election to be held in early June. The only problem is that he has come out strongly for the right to abortion on demand—an issue you strongly oppose.

What would you do? Why?

64. Moral Issues for Discussion: Parents/Teens

Part 1: Encircle **Y** if your response to this question is yes, **N** if it is no, and **?** if you are not sure.

Y N ? 1. Are some contemporary ways of dressing immoral?

Y N ? 2. Do parents have a right/duty to tell their teenage children how to dress?

Y N ? 3. Do parents have the right to charge their teens (who have a job) for room and board?

Y N ? 4. Are parents obligated to sacrifice to provide their children with a quality college education?

Y N ? 5. Do parents have the right to know if their teenager has obtained a birth-control device?

Y N ? 6. Should parents have the right to know if their teenage daughter has gone to an abortion clinic to request an abortion?

Y N ? 7. Would you want to know if your teenage children were engaged in premarital sex?

Y N ? 8. Do parents have the right to know how you spend money you have earned at a part-time job?

Y N ? 9. Do parents have the right to forbid their teens to associate with other teens of whom they disapprove?

Y N ? 10. Do parents have the right to know your exact whereabouts when you go out with friends on weekends?

Part 2: Discussion

1. Do parents expect too much from their teens today? Explain.

2. Discuss the five most important duties parents have toward their teenage children.

3. Discuss the five most important obligations teenage children have toward their parents.

4. Share your responses to the ten questions above.

65. Rationalization?

Morality means accepting responsibility for our own actions and attitudes. Yet, many times people try to disown their behavior, pretending that they didn't really do it or are not responsible for it. This is where *rationalization* sets in. Rationalization means making incorrect but self-serving excuses for our behavior, usually wrong behavior.

Gabriel Meurier (d. 1601) wrote, "He who excuses himself accuses himself." These are wise words. It seems to be part of human nature to take the easy way out, to blame our shortcomings on something or someone else.

Here is a list of comments. Some of them seem to be valid reasons for certain behavior. Others are clearly rationalizations. Check off those you believe are simply excuses for dodging responsibility.

_____ 1. "I didn't know what the speed limit was."

_____ 2. "I flunked the test because the teacher doesn't like me."

_____ 3. "I came in late because the car had a flat tire."

_____ 4. "I didn't give the derelict a dollar because I thought he'd spend it on a cheap bottle of wine."

_____ 5. "Everybody else was drinking so I did, too."

_____ 6. "I simply forgot about your birthday."

_____ 7. "Why go to the polls? What difference does one vote make anyhow?"

_____ 8. "I didn't realize he could make me so mad. When he started poking fun at my sister I just got violent."

_____ 9. "I got drunk because I didn't know my limit."

_____ 10. "So I littered. Big deal. There were no trash containers around."

■ discuss ■

1. What other facts would you like to know about each item to judge it more fairly?

2. Do you think we too easily try to rationalize our wrong behavior? Explain with examples.

3. What are some typical excuses your friends make when they perform poorly at athletics or academics? What is the funniest "line" you have heard?

66. Sin

Sin is a failure to love God above everything and our neighbor as ourselves. Whenever we sin, we have damaged human relationships. We have hurt others and ourselves.

Mortal sin involves serious matter and is done with knowledge and full consent of the will. It kills our love relationship.

Venial sin involves less serious matter or is done with insufficient knowledge or limited freedom.

Complete the following exercises individually. Then discuss the questions that follow:

Sin is more like... (circle the letter of your choice)

1. a. driving recklessly
   b. not going to the wake of a friend's mother

2. a. teasing a younger brother or sister
   b. lying to your parents about your whereabouts

3. a. reading a pornographic magazine
   b. gossiping about a classmate you don't like

4. a. drinking alcoholic beverages to excess
   b. cheating on a major exam

5. a. not responding to an appeal for the missions
   b. swearing

> Please judge the seriousness of the following actions:
> **M** = mortal sin; **V** = venial sin; **NS** = no sin.

_____ 1. stealing something worth $1,000
_____ 2. sexual relations between homosexuals
_____ 3. saying you love someone in order to gain sexual favors
_____ 4. failing to help someone at the scene of an accident
_____ 5. selling drugs to support an addiction
_____ 6. jealousy which leads to telling lies about a person

_____ 7. wantonly killing animals just for the fun of it

_____ 8. having a million dollars and not sharing any of it with the poor

---

■ *discuss* ■

What in your judgment makes something seriously wrong? What is the greatest personal sin being committed in today's world? What is the worst sin society in general seems to permit? Explain and give examples.

---

67. Still More Dilemmas: Living the Christian Life

Directions: Think about these cases against the background of Jesus' call to strive for perfection.

Suppose you are married and earn $70,000 per year. You are honest, hard-working, and pay your fair share of taxes. Your spouse is not employed; she is a full-time mother caring for your six children.

Because of your closeness to Jesus, you are wondering whether you should donate $20,000 of your salary each year to the poor. In doing so you will, in effect, be denying your family some nice amenities of life, things enjoyed by many of your children's friends. Is it right for you to be this generous at your family's expense?

Suppose you were a scientist working on the atomic bomb, and you had the presence of mind to foresee its terrible consequences. However, you also knew that tremendous knowledge concerning nuclear energy would be an outcome of your research. Would you have continued to work on the bomb?

If not, would you have tried to sabotage the efforts of your fellow scientists?

Should science continue its pursuit of mastery of creation? What if this pursuit risks destroying the environment and ultimately the human race?

You come home from a party one night only to discover that there is a terrible fire. You *might* be able to rescue either your ten-year-old brother or your father. Do you *have* to risk your own life to rescue them? Would you? If so, who would it be? Why?

You have been studying Christian morality in school for the past few months. Jesus' teaching of the Golden Rule—"Do unto others as you would have them do unto you"—has hit you like a sledgehammer. You have lent $100 to a friend. Now you are not so certain that you should ask for it back because you would certainly want her to forgive your debt if you were in the same place. What should you do? If you acted on the Golden Rule, you would never get ahead and everybody would take advantage of you. You ask yourself, "Is it impossible to live a Christian moral life?"

■ *discussion* ■

1. Can a true Christian live in the real world? Or are the demands too great?
2. How literally should we take the Golden Rule?
3. In living the Christian life, are we required to jeopardize our own personal safety if the situation calls for that?
4. Can a person be *too* generous?

section eight

Some Final Cases

68. Heroes or Fools?

Not long ago five farmers died in a manure pit trying to save one another. "What forced them down into the pit? It certainly wasn't fame or glory. It was love," said the minister to his Lutheran congregation, which crowded into the rural church to say farewell. The deceased included the sixty-five-year-old owner of the farm, his cousin (age sixty-three), his sons (ages thirty-seven and twenty-eight), and his grandson (age fifteen).

The five were overcome by methane fumes at the family's Michigan dairy farm. Apparently the owner's cousin went into the 12-foot-deep pit first—perhaps to clear a drain—and collapsed after breathing the fumes. Each one followed to rescue the man before, until all had died.

Decide: Check the statement that most closely reflects your thoughts about this case. Share and defend your choice.

_____ The four rescuers are all heroes. There is no greater love than a willingness to lay down your life so another may live.

_____ Other than the first rescuer, the other three were fools. Surely there must have been another way intelligent people could have gone about this rescue without endangering their own lives.

_____ All the rescuers were fools. No one is obligated to die for another.

■ *discuss* ■

1. Report details of any case similar to this that you have read about or seen reported on television.

2. Say you were the fifteen-year-old grandson and had witnessed what had happened to your older family members. What would you have done?

3. Would you be morally wrong if you did not go in after your family members? Explain.

69. Hit the Car?

Popular newspaper columnist Mike Royko once reported on this true story. One day a young woman was driving on one of Chicago's expressways. She was driving cautiously because the roads were icy and snow-covered. Out of nowhere, a green car sped by and sideswiped her. Her car went into a tailspin and came to rest in the path of an onrushing semi. At that moment time froze as her life passed before her.

The truck driver had one of two choices as he bore down on the helpless car: continue to go straight, inevitably plowing broadside into the woman; or cut sharply to the right, risking grave injury to himself and his bride of four months, who was in the truck with him.

As he related the story later, the truck driver said that he could see that the woman would be instantly killed if he continued on a straight course. Thus, he made a last-second decision to cut right. He smashed into a light pole, jack-knifed sideways and slid into a ditch on the side of the freeway. His brave, self-sacrificing act resulted in his sustaining several injured vertebrae and a collapsed lung. Unable to go to work, he had to wear a back brace for nine months. His wife emerged unscathed, but his truck was demolished.

The woman whose life he saved was extremely grateful.

The kicker to the story is what happened afterward. The state trooper told the truck driver he would have been better off had he hit the woman. He would not have wrecked his truck or damaged the light pole, and he would have escaped uninjured. The trooper informed him that he would have been within his rights had he hit her and that the insurance company would have paid for any damage done.

The trucker's employer also questioned why he did not hit the woman.

The police wrote up the accident report blaming the bad weather since they could not catch the green car, which had sped away.

The truck driver wondered aloud whether he did the right thing to avoid killing the woman. He spent his months of recovery thinking about what he did and what the police and his employer said.

1. Was the truck driver right or wrong in what he did? Explain.
2. Are the responses of the police and employer typical?
3. Did the truck driver have the *duty* to cut his wheels and risk his life and the life of his wife? Explain.
4. Have you ever gone out of your way to do something for somebody? If so, explain the example and describe your feelings afterward.
5. Has anyone ever called you a fool for doing something heroic?

70. Simulation: Jury

Scenario: The following simulation casts you as a member of a jury. You are to judge the degree of evil for each of the following situations. Your opinion, thought, and reflection are highly valued.

Part 1:

1. The following pages describe twelve situations, all of which harm human relationships. After each situation is a key word to help you remember the details of the story.

2. After reading each story, transcribe the key word under the column entitled "Key Words," which follows the situations. Mark in the space to the right a number from 1-7 to measure your *emotional* reaction to each situation. 1 represents the weakest emotional reaction, 7 the strongest. Use 2 through 6 to represent progressively stronger reactions. You may use the same number as often as you like. You may change your reactions as you go along. But remember, measure your *emotional* reaction.

3. After you have read and reacted to all the situations, please rank the four that evoked your strongest emotional response and the two that brought about your weakest reaction. Transcribe the key words in the column marked "E."

The Situations

1. It has come to your attention that a teacher at your school, married and the father of three children, has been accused of molesting a male student who graduated three years ago. **TEACHER**

2. A little boy, a neighborhood pest and brat, hates a certain elderly lady in the neighborhood for constantly yelling at him for playing on her lawn. To get even with her, he cuts the blooms off every one of her prize tulips. **TULIPS**

3. The woman in the previous story seeks to get revenge on the neighborhood brat. When his dog runs into her yard, she throws a rock at it, badly injuring one paw. **DOG**

4. A prominent news item in the Sunday paper reveals that the American government is actively supporting a dictator who systematically oppresses any church person who speaks out on land reform for the poor. **DICTATOR**

5. A close friend confides to you that he stayed home from school the other day. He disguised his voice and called in sick by claiming he was his father. Since both of his parents were at work, he was free to use the family car. He

did so and tells you he was involved in a near-fatal, hit-and-run accident. Thus far, neither the police nor his parents know of the crime. **ACCIDENT**

6. You recently have found out that a neighborhood youth got his girlfriend pregnant and then paid for an abortion. His reason was that her parents were ready to disown her and that he was not financially ready to marry her. **ABORTION**

7. A TV news item reveals that high-placed government officials have relaxed bank reform measures for their friends. They have accepted payoffs in exchange. **PAYOFF**

8. The newspaper reports that a group of reactionary racists bombed a Jewish synagogue in New York City as a protest for the government's support for Israel. Two old people and one child were killed and six others were injured. **SYNAGOGUE**

9. A neighbor girl who is in the third grade came home from school yesterday and told the family that her teacher, who is a man, kept her after school and, once they were alone, made sexual advances. **NEIGHBOR GIRL**

10. A factory owner of a large industrial chemical plant is losing money by using his antipollution equipment. So, at night when no one is watching, he opens the pollution control valves and allows the liquid pollutant by-products to be disposed of in a nearby stream. **POLLUTANTS**

11. A senior at your school was killed last week in a drunken-driving accident. His friend, who was driving, escaped without injury. Both had been drinking. **ACCIDENT**

12. Recently you purchased a good compact disc player. You had been saving for it for quite some time and paid cash for it. Unfortunately, on your way home from the store, you stopped off to run a few more errands. While doing your other shopping, someone broke into the car and stole your recent purchase. Unfortunately, the deductible on your parents' insurance policy is too high to cover the loss. **CD PLAYER**

KEY WORDS   **RANK**

1. _____ ____   7. _____ ____

2. _____ ____   8. _____ ____

3. _____ ____   9. _____ ____

4. _____ ____   10. _____ ____

5. _____ ____   11. _____ ____

6. _____ ____   12. _____ ____

E	R (Part 2)
1. _____	1. _____
2. _____	2. _____
3. _____	3. _____
4. _____	4. _____
11. _____	11. _____
12. _____	12. _____

Part 2:

1. Form small groups of six.

2. Compare your initial rankings.

3. Now, let the *group* rerank the top four and bottom two. This time react as though you could remove all emotion from your consideration. Judge on a *rational* basis alone. In other words, on the basis of reason, which of these situations *should* evoke the strongest reactions? the weakest? Recopy these key words in the column marked "R."

4. Your group should arrive at a consensus in about fifteen minutes.

Part 3:

1. If possible, form a circle, staying with your group.

2. Each group in turn should share its rankings from column "R." A brief statement of reasons for the choices made should be given at this time.

3. After each group has reported, *discuss* the following questions:

   a. Did your small group come to any different conclusions using *reason* alone than you did using *emotion*? If so, why? If not, why not?

   b. Was this a difficult task to do? Is it difficult for a human being to judge a situation without any emotional consideration?

   c. What made one situation more serious than another? (the number of people? the kind of people? the kind of crime? the role of the individual? etc.)

   d. What priorities did your group set in coming to consensus? Were they different from those of another group?

   e. How much did the *intention* of the characters in the story affect your decisions? the *circumstances*? the *action* itself?

   f. What assumptions did you make about each story? Did these change any of your choices?

   g. How do you think Jesus would rank these situations? Do you have any evidence to support your choice?

h. Can you find evidence in the New Testament that shows Jesus was not happy with the following:

- hypocrisy
- lack of respect for human life
- failure to identify each person as neighbor
- harm performed to the outcast and the defenseless victim, such as children